BLACKSTONE'S POLICE

EVIDENCE & PROCEDURE

BLACKSTONE'S POLICE

EVIDENCE & PROCEDURE

First Edition

Huw Smart and
John Watson

Consultant Editor:
Fraser Sampson

OXFORD
UNIVERSITY PRESS

OXFORD

UNIVERSITY PRESS

Great Clarendon Street, Oxford OX2 6DP

Oxford University Press is a department of the University of Oxford.
It furthers the University's objective of excellence in research, scholarship,
and education by publishing worldwide in

Oxford NewYork

Athens Auckland Bangkok Bogotá Buenos Aires Cape Town
Chennai Dar es Salaam Delhi Florence Hong Kong Istanbul Karachi
Kolkata Kuala Lumpur Madrid Melbourne Mexico City Mumbai Nairobi
Paris São Paulo Shanghai Singapore Taipei Tokyo Toronto Warsaw

with associated companies in Berlin Ibadan

Oxford is a registered trade mark of Oxford University Press
in the UK and certain other countries

Published in the United States
by Oxford University Press Inc., New York

A Blackstone Press Book

British Library Cataloguing in Publication Data

Data available

Library of Congress Cataloging in Publication Data

Data available

ISBN 1-84174-293-7

1 3 5 7 9 10 8 6 4 2

Typeset by Style Photosetting Limited, Mayfield, East Sussex
Printed in Great Britain
on acid-free paper by
Ashford Colour Press Limited, Gosport, Hampshire

CONTENTS

INTRODUCTION

Before you get into the detail of this book, there are two myths about Multiple Choice Questions (MCQs) that we need to get out of the way right at the start:

1. that they are easy to answer
2. that they are easy to write

Take one look at a professionally designed and properly developed exam paper such as those used by the Police Promotion Examinations Board or the National Board of Medical Examiners in the US and the first myth collapses straight away. Contrary to what some people believe, MCQs are not an easy solution for examiners and not a 'multiple-guess' soft option for examinees.

That is not to say that *all* MCQs are taxing, or even testing — in the psychometric sense. If MCQs are to have any real value at all, they need to be carefully designed and follow some agreed basic rules.

And this leads us to myth number 2.

It is widely assumed by many people and educational organisations that anyone with the knowledge of a subject can write MCQs. You need only look at how few MCQ writing courses are offered by training providers in the UK to see just how far this myth is believed. Similarly, you need only to have a go at a few badly designed MCQs to realise that it *is* a myth none the less. Writing bad MCQs is easy; writing good ones is no easier than answering them!

As with many things, the design of MCQs benefits considerably from time, training and experience. Many MCQ writers fall easily and often unwittingly into the trap of making their questions too hard, too easy or too obscure, or completely different from the type of question that you will eventually encounter in your own particular exam. Others seem to use the MCQ as a way to catch people out or to show how smart they, the authors, are (or think they are).

There are several purposes for which MCQs are very useful. The first is in producing a reliable, valid and fair test of knowledge and understanding across a wide range of subject matter. Another is an aid to study, preparation and revision for such examinations and tests. The differences in objective mean that there are slight differences in the rules that the MCQ writers follow. Whereas the design of fully validated MCQs to be used in high stakes examinations which will effectively determine who passes and who fails have very strict guidelines as to construction, content and style, less stringent rules apply to MCQs that are being used for teaching and revision. For that reason, there may be types of MCQ that are appropriate in the latter setting which would not be used in the former. However, in developing the MCQs for this book, the authors have tried to follow the fundamental rules of MCQ design but they would not claim to have replicated the level of psychometric rigour that is — and has to be — adopted by the type of examining bodies referred to above.

These MCQs are designed to reinforce your knowledge and understanding, to highlight any gaps or weaknesses in that knowledge and understanding and to help focus your revision of the relevant topics.

I hope that we have achieved that aim.

Good luck!

ACKNOWLEDGEMENTS

As qualified police trainers, we have written this book to complement *Blackstone's Police Manuals* and to provide a source of improving knowledge of police-related legislation. It is important to recognise that full study of the relevant chapters in the *Police Manuals* is recommended before attempting the Questions and Answers.

Particular attention should be paid to **Answers** section and students should always ask themselves, 'Why did I get the question wrong?' and just as importantly 'Why did I get the question right'. Combining the information gained from self-questioning and the information contained in the **Answers** section should lead to a greater understanding of the subject matter.

We wish to thank Alistair MacQueen for his faith, Heather Saward for pulling it all together and Fraser Sampson for his words of wisdom. Thanks also to Jane Kavanagh at Oxford University Press for her continuing support of the project.

Huw would like to thank Julie for her patience and understanding during long evenings and weekends of work, Ian, Debbie, Theresa and Vince at Detail Technologies Limited for all their hard work.

John would like to thank Sue for her patience and understanding during long evenings and weekends of work and remind David, Catherine and Andrew that Daddy is not just the man who sits in the corner working on his computer.

1 SUMMONSES AND WARRANTS

STUDY PREPARATION

A nice gentle start to the subject. And, appropriately, it's the way in which prosecutions are started. Laying informations and securing the attendance of witnesses, defendants and evidence are basic mechanics of the criminal justice procedure. As with other areas of practical relevance, this means that they will be of interest to trainers and examiners.

QUESTIONS

Question 1

In relation to the issuing of a summons and a warrant to commit to prison, which of the following is true?

[A] A justices' clerk can issue either the warrant or the summons.
[B] A justices' clerk can issue the summons only.
[C] A justices' clerk can issue the warrant only.
[D] A justices' clerk cannot issue either the warrant or the summons.

Question 2

O'KELLY wishes to take action to have a dangerous dog destroyed by attending at the local magistrates' court and obtaining a destruction order under s. 2 of the Dogs Act 1871.

How should O'KELLY proceed in this matter?

[A] By laying an information for the issue of a summons for the dog's owner to attend.
[B] By laying an information for the issue of a warrant for the dog's owner to attend.
[C] By laying a written complaint before the magistrate.
[D] By laying a verbal complaint before the magistrate.

Question 3

In relation to laying an information with regard to obtaining a summons for an offence of dangerous driving, which of the following is correct?

[A] The information must be in writing and substantiated on oath.
[B] The information must be made orally, but must be substantiated on oath.
[C] The information can be made orally or in writing, but must be substantiated on oath.
[D] The information can be made orally or in writing and no oath is required.

Question 4

RUBIN has been caught speeding by a mobile speed enforcement camera. His speed was more then twice the legal limit and the police force in whose area the speeding offence was committed wishes to issue a summons against him.

Is it in order for the force to lay an information to obtain a summons?

[A] Yes, provided the name of the actual force concerned is on the information.
[B] Yes, as a 'person' includes 'a body of persons corporate or unincorporate'.
[C] No, as it must be a named, actual person who lays the information.
[D] No, as it is the prosecutor or his counsel only who lays the information.

Question 5

Constable DURKIN has stopped a serving officer of the British Army for failing to comply with a red traffic signal. The Army officer was driving a vehicle that belongs to the British Army and has Army index plates. Constable DURKIN is unsure as to whether she can proceed by way of summons.

In relation to a member of the armed forces, which of the following is generally true?

[A] Being served on the individual officer concerned, a summons is effected.
[B] Being served on the individual officer concerned, as well as his or her commanding officer, a summons is effected.
[C] Being served on the individual officer's commanding officer, a summons is effected.
[D] A summons cannot be served on a serving officer of the British Army, whilst driving an army vehicle.

Question 6

WONG was reported by a police officer for careless driving. The prosecutor conceded that the evidence was weak and took time to consider the facts. Having not reached a firm decision on whether to take proceedings, the prosecutor laid the information before the court, simply to keep his options open. The information was laid one day within a six-month period since the incident. However, two months elapsed before the summons was actually served on WONG. The offence carries a statute bar of six months.

Should the magistrates allow the case to go ahead?

[A] Yes, the information was laid within the six-month period.
[B] Yes, the summons was served within six months of the information being laid.
[C] No, as the summons was not issued within the six-month period.
[D] No, owing to an abuse of the process of the court.

Question 7

Constable SIMPSON was executing a warrant for non-payment of court fines at GEOGHAN'S home address. The warrant is held at the police station which is half a mile away. The door is opened by GEOGHAN who claims he has no money and will happily go with the officer. The officer arrests him under the terms of the warrant and takes him to the police station.

Is this arrest lawful?

[A] No, the officer is not in possession of the warrant, the station is too far away.
[B] No, as the officer should have *all* such warrants in *physical* possession.
[C] Yes, as GEOGHAN has no money to pay, there is no need to have the warrant.
[D] Yes, as possession has been held to include where the warrant was nearby at the station.

Question 8

Constable McGEE is a serving officer in a Welsh police force, but Scottish in origin. Before going on leave he reads a PNC broadcast about an arrest warrant for an offence issued in Glasgow, it concerns a student he was at University with who he knows well. Whilst on holiday on the south coast of England, he sees his friend against whom the warrant was issued.

Can he arrest his friend by executing the warrant?

[A] Yes, a warrant issued in Scotland can be executed in England or Wales by a constable.
[B] Yes, but only if the Scottish offence corresponds with an English law offence.
[C] No, the warrant would have to be in his possession to arrest in England.
[D] No, because he is not acting within his own force area.

Question 9

DICKERSON is a civilian enforcement officer employed by the local court and authorised in the prescribed manner. DICKERSON is executing a distress warrant at an address when he notices RYAN, for whom he knows an arrest warrant has been issued. DICKERSON does not have this warrant in his possession.

Can DICKERSON execute the warrant for arrest?

[A] Yes, a civilian enforcement officer can execute any warrant.
[B] Yes, an arrest warrant is one that can be executed by a civilian enforcement officer.
[C] No, a civilian enforcement officer must have possession of an arrest warrant.
[D] No, a civilian enforcement officer cannot execute an arrest warrant.

ANSWERS

Question 1

Answer **B** — A summons means a written order issued by a magistrate or a magistrates' (justices') clerk, on behalf of the magistrate. This means a justices' clerk can issue a summons and therefore answer D is incorrect, as is answer C. Unlike the issue of a summons, the justices' clerk is not allowed to issue any type of warrant; the information has to be made to a justice and answer A is therefore incorrect.

Question 2

Answer **D** — A complaint is a verbal allegation made before a magistrate to the effect that a person has committed a breach of the law not being a criminal offence and answer C is therefore incorrect. Acts of Parliament sometimes enact that proceedings are to be taken by way of complaint and s. 2 of the Dogs Act 1871 is such an enactment, i.e. where proceedings instituted by 'information' are invalid and answers A and B are therefore incorrect.

Question 3

Answer **D** — Rule 4(2) of the Magistrates' Courts Rules 1981 (SI 1981 No. 552) provides that an information (an allegation that someone has committed an offence) may be laid orally or in writing and answers A and B are therefore incorrect. The information need not be given on oath and answer C is therefore incorrect.

Question 4

Answer **C** — By r. 4(1) of the Magistrates' Courts Rules 1981, 'An information may be laid . . . by the prosecutor . . . or by his counsel or solicitor or other person authorised in that behalf' and answer D is therefore incorrect. However, an information may not be laid on behalf of an unincorporated association, such as a police force — answer A is therefore incorrect. Also, since the definition of 'person' in the Interpretation Act 1978 as including a 'body of persons corporate or unincorporate' was not intended to apply to the laying of informations (*Rubin* v *DPP* [1990] 2 QB 80), answer B is incorrect. It follows that an information must be laid by a named, actual person and must disclose the identity of that person. This could be met by laying informations in the name of the Chief Constable (who *is* a body corporate.)

Question 5

Answer **B** — Generally the service of a summons on a member of the armed forces is effected by it being served on the individual officer concerned, as well as his or her commanding officer in the case of the army and RAF personnel and answers A, C and D are therefore incorrect. If the person concerned serves in the Royal Navy or the Royal Marines, the commanding officer of a ship or other establishment is the other relevant person for the summons to be served on.

Question 6

Answer **D** — Deliberate delay of laying an information to obtain a summons has been considered by the courts. The leading authority on this is *R v Brentford Justices, ex parte Wong* [1981] QB 445. An information against Wong for careless driving was laid one day within the six-month period permitted by s. 127 of the Magistrates' Courts Act 1980. The prosecutor conceded that he had not then reached a firm decision on whether to take proceedings, but had laid the information simply to keep his options open. Having obtained a summons, there was a further delay and it was several months before the summons was actually served. The magistrates indicated sympathy with the defence argument that the prosecution delay was improper but continued with the case. The Divisional Court, in considering the facts, held that the magistrates did have discretion to decline hearing the case if there had been an abuse of process, and what happened in this case could, and should, be regarded as an abuse of process and proceedings should have been stayed. Consequently, answers A, B and C are incorrect.

Question 7

Answer **A** — A warrant to which s. 125(3) of the Magistrates' Courts Act 1980 applies, is a warrant to arrest a person in connection with an offence or for certain offences pertaining to the armed forces, or under s. 18(4) of the Domestic Proceedings and Magistrates' Courts Act 1978 (protection of parties to the marriage and children of the family), and under s. 55, 76, 93 or 97 of the 1980 Act itself. Such a warrant may be executed by a constable even though it is not in his or her possession at the time. It must be shown to the person arrested, if he or she demands it, as soon as practicable.

This does, however, not include arrest for a civil proceeding such as non-payment of a fine which must be in the officer's possession (*R* v

Peacock (1989) 153 JP 199). The purpose of requiring the constable to have the warrant in his or her possession is so that the person concerned can pay the fine and buy his or her freedom. This duty is not negated simply because the offender has no money and answer C is therefore incorrect. 'Possession' has been held to include a warrant which was in a police car approximately 60 yards away (*R* v *Purdy* [1974] 3 All ER 465) and answer B is therefore incorrect. Note, however, it is not in the officer's possession when it was at a police station half a mile away and answer D is therefore incorrect. Note that the police rarely deal with these warrants as the courts tend to deal with them themselves.

Question 8

Answer **D** — A warrant issued in Scotland or Northern Ireland for the arrest of a person charged with an offence may be executed in England or Wales (s. 38(1) of the Criminal Law Act 1977), and need not be in the possession of the officer, s. 125(3) of the Magistrates' Courts Act 1980 applies by virtue of s. 38(1) of the 1977 Act (answer C is therefore incorrect). The offence for which the warrant was issued does not require a corresponding English offence and answer B is therefore incorrect (although this is the case for some Republic of Ireland warrants). The only condition applied to the constable making the arrest in England and Wales is that he or she must be acting within his or her police area and answer A is therefore incorrect.

Question 9

Answer **B** — Section 92 of the Access to Justice 1999 enables certain warrants to be executed in England and Wales by a civilian enforcement officer provided he or she has been authorised in the prescribed manner and answer D is therefore incorrect. However, this does not extend to all warrants and answer A is therefore incorrect. An arrest warrant is one of those that can be executed by a civilian enforcement officer, but it does not stipulate that the warrant has to be in the officer's possession and answer C is therefore incorrect.

2　BAIL

STUDY PREPARATION

In terms of constitutional powers the granting — and more importantly the denial — of bail is an area of fundamental importance. While there are lots of areas where tenuous human rights arguments have been raised since the 1998 Act was introduced, this one is for real. This area raises lots of questions about an individual's human rights — and therefore potentially lots of questions in exam papers.

For sergeants and inspectors it is vital to know the extent of powers that exist to restrict or deny a person's bail. Practically this area is sometimes misunderstood, with many police officers (and lawyers) confusing the areas which will permit the police and courts to restrict a person's bail or to deny it all together.

QUESTIONS

Question 1

Officers have arrested McLAREN for an offence of theft and place him before the custody officer. The custody officer decides that, although further enquiries are necessary, there is currently insufficient evidence to charge and that there are no grounds to detain McLAREN.

In relation to releasing McLAREN, what can the custody officer do?

[A] She can release McLAREN on bail, which must be unconditional.
[B] She can release McLAREN on bail, which can have conditions.
[C] She cannot release McLAREN on bail in cases where there is insufficient evidence to charge.
[D] She cannot release McLAREN on bail where there are no grounds for detention.

Question 2

When a person is charged at a police station, the custody officer must make a decision about bail.

In relation to this decision and any representations made, which of the following is true?

[A] Only the person charged is allowed to make representations prior to the decision being made.
[B] If the person is legally represented, only the solicitor is allowed to make representations prior to the decision being made.
[C] Either the person charged or a solicitor is allowed to make representations prior to the decision being made.
[D] The custody officer does not need to listen to representations from anyone prior to the decision being made.

Question 3

CABALLERO was tried and convicted for an offence of manslaughter 10 years ago, for which he was *not* given a prison sentence due to the circumstances of the case. CABALLERO has recently been arrested for murder. However, CABALLERO has been charged with manslaughter again. The custody officer is considering bail.

Which of the following is true?

[A] CABALLERO cannot be given bail, unless he shows exceptional circumstances to justify it.

[B] CABALLERO cannot be given bail in any circumstances, as he has previously been convicted of a manslaughter offence.

[C] CABALLERO should be bailed, unless one of the grounds under s. 38(1) of the Police and Criminal Evidence Act 1984 applies.

[D] CABALLERO should be granted bail only if there are exceptional circumstances justifying it.

Question 4

The custody officer is considering whether SHILLITOE, having been charged with an offence of burglary, should be granted bail. The investigating officer believes that bail should be refused, as she suspects that SHILLITOE will commit further offences. The investigating officer believes this because SHILLITOE has previously offended whilst on bail.

Is the previous offending on bail relevant to the custody officer's decision?

[A] No, any reasonable grounds for refusing bail cannot be gained from previous incidents.

[B] No, 'commission of further offences' relates to non-imprisonable offences only.

[C] Yes, provided those offences committed on bail were burglary offences.

[D] Yes, provided it is considered with other factors, e.g. the strength of the evidence.

Question 5

MILLIGAN is appearing in court on a charge of murder, and the court is going to grant bail. There have been no formal reports on MILLIGAN'S mental condition, and the prosecution have asked that, as a condition of the bail, the magistrates direct that MILLIGAN undergo an examination for the purpose of obtaining such a report.

Which of the following statements is true?

[A] The prosecution's application must be granted.
[B] The prosecution's application can be granted if the court considers it an appropriate condition.
[C] The prosecution's application cannot be granted as this is not a condition of bail.
[D] The prosecution's application cannot be granted as medical reports can be sought only after conviction.

Question 6

YOUSEL has been released from police custody on bail, with conditions to report to the police station every Wednesday at 9 pm and not to interfere with prosecution witnesses. YOUSEL wishes to have the conditions varied so he does not have to report to the police station.

Which of the following statements is true?

[A] YOUSEL must speak to the actual custody officer who bailed him.
[B] YOUSEL can speak to any custody officer at any station.
[C] YOUSEL risks having his conditions made more onerous by such a request.
[D] YOUSEL must be accompanied by his solicitor in making such a request.

Question 7

When imposing bail conditions on a person accused of an offence, can a custody officer demand the surrender of the accused's passport?

[A] Yes, provided the custody officer thinks this to be an appropriate condition in the circumstances.
[B] Yes, provided there is a real and substantive risk that the accused will abscond.
[C] No, the European courts have ruled that this infringes a person's human rights.
[D] No, such a condition can be imposed only by a magistrate or judge.

Question 8

If an accused has provided a surety (MARKS) to secure his surrender to custody, and then has failed to appear at court, what must MARKS prove in order to not forfeit his recognisance?

[A] That MARKS took all possible steps to ensure that the accused attended court.
[B] That MARKS informed the police, verbally, that the accused was likely not to turn up.
[C] That MARKS took reasonable steps to ensure that the accused attended court.
[D] That MARKS had not been involved in the accused's non-appearance.

Question 9

SULLY is an eleven-year-old boy charged with burglary. There are clear grounds for the custody officer to refuse bail to prevent further offending. There is no secure local authority accommodation available, and the only accommodation the local authority can provide would be easy to escape from.

In relation to detaining SULLY at the police station, which of the following is true?

[A]   SULLY can be detained as no secure accommodation is available.
[B]   SULLY can be detained provided there would be a risk to the public by placing him in the insecure accommodation.
[C]   SULLY can be detained provided the custody officer certifies that it would have been impractical to find local authority accommodation.
[D]   SULLY can be detained provided the custody officer certifies that it would have been impractical for him to be taken into local authority care.

Question 10

A custody officer must review the detention of a person detained, after bail has been refused. Following the decision to refuse bail, within how many hours should the custody officer review the person's continued detention?

[A]   Within six hours of the decision to refuse bail, and the question of bail should now be reconsidered.
[B]   Within nine hours of the decision to refuse bail, and the question of bail should now be reconsidered.
[C]   Within six hours of the decision to refuse bail, however the question of bail does not arise during this review.
[D]   Within nine hours of the decision to refuse bail, however the question of bail does not arise during this review.

Question 11

BREEZE was on unconditional bail on a charge of assault. The magistrates' court granted bail for a period of four weeks. BREEZE failed to appear and a warrant was issued. He was arrested three weeks later and taken before the court. When he gave evidence relating to a charge of absconding, BREEZE stated he had been in hospital at the time of the court date and left hospital a week later. He also stated he had not been given a copy of the court record of the date of his next appearance.

In relation to BREEZE's potential offence of absconding, which of the following is true?

[A] BREEZE did not commit the offence as he had reasonable cause not to surrender.
[B] BREEZE did not commit the offence because he did not receive a copy of the court record.
[C] BREEZE still committed the offence even though he had reasonable cause.
[D] BREEZE committed the offence simply by failing to appear in the first place.

Question 12

Constable AKANJI was on duty at a briefing for the 2 pm–10 pm shift. During the briefing, her sergeant says that it was believed that BOLTON had failed to attend at the police station last week to answer police bail in answer to an allegation of theft. Whilst on patrol, Constable AKANJI sees BOLTON walking down the street, and is considering arresting him.

Which of the following statements is true?

[A] The officer can arrest BOLTON on reasonable suspicion that he 'failed to appear', and she will be arresting him for theft.
[B] The officer can arrest BOLTON on reasonable suspicion that he 'failed to appear', and she will be arresting him for that offence.
[C] The officer cannot arrest BOLTON until she confirms that he did not attend the police station as required.
[D] The officer cannot arrest BOLTON unless there is new evidence in relation to the theft.

Question 13

BALDWIN was on bail to attend at a magistrates' court at a date in the future. Constable NEWELL received firm evidence that BALDWIN was not going to surrender, but was certain to abscond. Constable NEWELL arrested BALDWIN at 11.20 am, on Monday, under s. 7(3), Bail Act 1976 and detention was authorised at 11.50 am. BALDWIN was taken to court at 10 am on Tuesday and appeared before a justice of the peace at 12 noon. The justice is of the opinion that BALDWIN will fail to surrender in the future.

In relation to what the justice may do next, which of the following is true?

[A]   He may remand BALDWIN in custody as he was brought to court within 24 hours of detention being authorised.

[B]   He may remand BALDWIN in custody as he was brought to court within 24 hours of the time he was arrested.

[C]   He may *not* remand BALDWIN in custody as he was not put before a justice within 24 hours of detention being authorised.

[D]   He may *not* remand BALDWIN in custody as he was not put before a justice within 24 hours of the time he was arrested.

Question 14

GABBIADINI has been convicted at a magistrates' court for an offence of taking a conveyance contrary to s. 12 of the Theft Act 1968. The magistrate is adjourning the case for sentencing reports indicating that she considers it 'serious enough' to demand a custodial sentence. Believing bail would not be granted, the prosecution made no application to oppose bail. The magistrate granted bail, and the prosecution wish to appeal against that decision to a judge of the Crown Court, and they give oral notice of that intention.

In relation to this appeal, which of the following is true?

[A] The appeal must be made within 48 hours of the time of the oral notice and the accused must be released on bail pending the appeal.
[B] The appeal does not apply to an offence of taking a conveyance as it does not carry a sentence of five years' imprisonment or more.
[C] The prosecution cannot appeal, because they did not oppose bail before it was granted.
[D] The prosecution can make the appeal, even though they did not oppose bail before it was granted.

Question 15

WHITE has been charged with several serious offences. The custody officer is deciding whether to grant bail or not, and needs to be aware of and give consideration to the rights and freedoms guaranteed under the European Convention on Human Rights when reaching that decision. There is, however, no evidence that WHITE has previously interfered with the course of justice while previously on bail.

In relation to the grounds on which to refuse bail, which of the following is true?

[A] The fact that the person had *not* previously 'interfered with the course of justice' whilst on bail would not help to justify remanding in custody.

[B] The serious nature of the offences charged alone will be sufficient reason when considering 'fear of absconding' to justify remanding him in custody.

[C] Any previous offences need not be comparable with the offence charged when considering 'the prevention of crime' to justify remanding him in custody.

[D] The fact there may be a public reaction that threatens 'the preservation of public order' to a release on bail would not help to justify remanding him in custody.

ANSWERS

Question 1

Answer **A**— The meaning of 'bail in criminal proceedings' is contained in s. 1 of the Bail Act 1976 which states:

> (1)   In this Act 'bail in criminal proceedings' means—
> (a)   bail grantable in or in connection with proceedings for an offence to a person who is accused or convicted of the offence, or
> (b)   bail grantable in connection with an offence to a person who is under arrest for the offence or for whose arrest for the offence a warrant (endorsed for bail) is being issued.

This is further endorsed by by s. 1(6) which states:

> Bail in criminal proceedings shall be granted (and in particular shall be granted unconditionally or conditionally), in accordance with this Act.

As the person, although not charged, has clearly been released 'in criminal proceedings', bail can be granted and answers C and D are therefore incorrect. Although it can be granted conditionally, answer B is incorrect because s. 47(1A) of the Police and Criminal Evidence Act 1984 states that where a person is bailed without being charged the custody officer cannot impose conditions on that bail.

Question 2

Answer **C** — This is a review of the person's detention and therefore, to comply with the Police and Criminal Evidence Act 1984, the person or his or her legal representative should be given an opportunity to make representations to the custody officer prior to that officer's decision whether or not to grant bail. The review should be conducted with regard to PACE Code C, paras 15.1 to 15.6. Note that if the detained person was a juvenile, the opportunity to make representations should be extended to the 'appropriate adult'.

As it is either the person or his or her solicitor who can make representations, answers A and B are therefore incorrect. Also, the custody officer has to allow opportunities for representations to be made and answer D is therefore incorrect.

Question 3

Answer **C** — Section 25 of the Criminal Justice and Public Order Act 1994 deals with the issue of bail for those charged with certain offences such as manslaughter. Generally speaking, a person charged with manslaughter should not be given bail if he or she has a previous conviction for that offence, unless there are exceptional circumstances for granting bail and answer B is therefore incorrect. Note there is, however, a caveat where the previous conviction is manslaughter, as it says in s. 25(3) 'in the case of a previous conviction for manslaughter or of culpable homicide, if he was then sentenced to imprisonment'. As this was not the case, the 'exceptional circumstances' do not apply, and Caballero must be granted bail unless one of the grounds under s. 38(1) of Police and Criminal Evidence Act 1984 apply and answers A and D are therefore incorrect.

Question 4

Answer **D** — Section 38(1) of the Police and Criminal Evidence Act 1984 provides that a custody officer need not grant bail if there are reasonable grounds for believing that bail should be refused to prevent the accused, among other things, committing other offence(s). The custody officer should give due weight to whether the accused had committed offences when previously on bail (therefore answer A is incorrect) and also other factors. These factors are:

- the nature and seriousness of the offence and the probable method of dealing with the offender for it;
- the character, antecedents, associations and community ties of the accused;
- the accused's 'record' for having answered bail in the past;
- the strength of the evidence against the accused.

Although there are grounds for refusing bail that relate to non-imprisonable offences only, the one relating to 'commission of further offences' relates to imprisonable offences only (i.e. burglary) and therefore answer B is incorrect. The previous offending is not specific to the offence currently charged, and would therefore relate to any offence and therefore answer C is incorrect — it is information which should be taken as a factor by the custody officer.

Question 5

Answer **A** — The general provisions as to bail are contained in s. 3 of the Bail Act 1976. Section 3(6A) deals with the court granting bail to a person accused of murder, it states:

In the case of a person accused of murder the court granting bail shall, unless it considers that satisfactory reports on his mental condition have already been obtained, impose as conditions of bail—

(a)　a requirement that the accused shall undergo examination by two medical practitioners for the purpose of enabling such reports to be prepared; and

(b)　a requirement that he shall for that purpose attend such an institution or place as the court directs and comply with any other directions which may be given to him for that purpose by either of those practitioners.

As can be seen, if bail is to be granted, the court is under a statutory obligation to impose such a condition and not only if it is appropriate and therefore answer B is incorrect. As it is the law, it is a condition of bail and therefore answer C is incorrect. Although requests for medical reports can be sought following conviction, they *must* be requested where the person is bailed, and as no such report has already been obtained, answer D is therefore incorrect.

Question 6

Answer **C** — Section 3A of the Bail Act 1976 applies to bail granted by a custody officer. In relation to varying imposed bail conditions, it states:

Where a custody officer has granted bail in criminal proceedings he or another custody officer serving at the same police station may, at the request of the person to whom it was granted, vary the conditions of bail; and in doing so he may impose conditions or more onerous conditions.

Yousel must visit the police station where the original conditions were imposed and therefore answer B is incorrect. However, any custody officer can be consulted and therefore answer A is incorrect. Section 3A does not obligate the presence of a legal representative, therefore answer D is incorrect. The legislation allows Yousel the opportunity to have the bail conditions varied, but in doing so he risks the imposition of more onerous conditions.

Question 7

Answer **B** — Under s. 3A of the Bail Act 1976, conditions can be imposed where it is necessary to do so for the purpose of preventing a person from:

• failing to surrender to custody, or

- committing an offence while on bail, or
- interfering with witnesses or otherwise obstructing the course of justice, whether in relation to himself or any other person.

One of those conditions is that of the accused having to surrender his passport, and this is available to both the court and the custody officer and therefore answer D is incorrect. In making such a decision, the custody officer has to take into account the punitive nature of any conditions imposed and can only place conditions where there is a 'real' risk of the accused absconding. It would not be sufficient to merely think it was appropriate, and must be based on 'a real and not a fanciful risk' (R v Mansfield Justices, ex parte Sharkey [1985] QB 613) and therefore answer A is incorrect. Any imposition of bail, with or without conditions, amounts to an interference with a person's rights under the European Convention on Human Rights and the European Court and Commission has examined the question of bail. Their approach generally is that an accused person should be released unconditionally unless factors that would otherwise lead to a refusal of bail can be met by imposing bail conditions. Against this background, the European Court has accepted that the surrender of a passport is a legitimate condition (Schmid v Austria (1985) 44 DR 195) and therefore answer C is incorrect.

Question 8

Answer **C** — Regulation 21 of the Crown Court Rules 1982 empowers the court to forfeit a surety's recognisance if there has been default in performing the obligations imposed. However, in R v Warwick Crown Court, ex parte Smalley [1987] 1 WLR 237, it was held there is no requirement of proof that any blame is attached to the surety for the accused's non-appearance and therefore answer D is incorrect. It is also not necessary for the surety to show that he took all possible steps to ensure the appearance of the accused and therefore answer A is incorrect. If the surety had taken all *reasonable* steps to ensure attendance, but the accused nevertheless let him down, the recognisance ought not to be forfeited (R v York Crown Court, ex parte Coleman (1987) 86 Cr App R 151). Part of those reasonable steps might well be notifying the police that the accused is unlikely to surrender to custody. However, such notification must be in writing and therefore answer B is incorrect.

Question 9

Answer **D** — A custody officer who authorises an arrested juvenile to be kept in police custody must secure that the arrested juvenile is moved to local authority accommodation unless he or she certifies that, by reason of such circumstances as are specified in the certificate, it is impracticable to do so or that, in the case of a juvenile who has attained the age of 12, that no secure accommodation is available *and* that keeping in other local authority accommodation would not be adequate to protect the public from serious harm from him (s. 38(6) of the Police and Criminal Evidence Act 1984). PACE Code C, Note 16B clearly states:

> The availability of secure accommodation is only a factor in relation to a juvenile aged 12 or over when the local authority accommodation would not be adequate to protect the public from serious harm from the juvenile.

As Sully is only 11 years of age, answers A and B are incorrect. Note 16B also states 'the lack of secure local authority accommodation shall not make it impracticable for the custody officer to transfer him'. This means that unless the exception applies the custody officer must physically hand him over to the care of the local authority. However, this does not apply to Sully who is only 11 years' old and therefore answer C is incorrect.

Question 10

Answer **B** — This review is exactly the same format as that carried out by an Inspector prior to charging, i.e. a review of the person's continued detention. The two times under s. 40 of the Police and Criminal Evidence Act 1984 are six hours and nine hours, the six-hour review coming after the detention was first authorised, and any subsequent reviews coming within nine hours of that review. This means any 'custody officer's review' must be within nine hours of any previous review and therefore answers A and C are incorrect. In considering the continued detention of a person, the custody officer must consider bail. Where, for instance, the grounds for refusing bail no longer apply, the person should be released on bail and, therefore answer D is incorrect.

Question 11

Answer **C** — Section 6 of the Bail Act 1976, creates the offence of absconding. By s. 6(1), if a person released on bail fails without reasonable cause to surrender to custody, he is guilty of an offence. The burden of showing reasonable cause is on the accused (s. 6(3)). Moreover, a person who had reasonable cause for failing to surrender on the appointed day nevertheless commits an offence if he fails to surrender *as soon after the appointed time as is reasonably practicable* (s. 6(2)). The fact that Breeze did not surrender to the court until being arrested means that although he had reasonable cause, he failed to surrender and therefore still commits the offence (answer A is incorrect). The offence is not absolute and is not committed simply by failing to surrender to custody and therefore answer D is incorrect. Section 6(4) of the 1976 Act states:

> A failure to give a person granted bail in criminal proceedings a copy of the record of the decision shall not constitute a reasonable cause for that person's failure to surrender to custody.

Therefore answer B is incorrect.

Question 12

Answer **C** — There are occasions where a person who has been bailed to return to a police station at a later date may be arrested without warrant. These occasions are dealt with by s. 46A of the Police and Criminal Evidence Act 1984 and s. 7 of the Bail Act 1976. Where a suspect, bailed from the police station under s. 37(2) of the 1984 Act on condition that he or she re-attend at the police station on a later date fails to do so, he or she may be arrested without warrant (s. 46A) and therefore answer D is incorrect. The offence for which the person is arrested is the offence for which he or she was originally arrested. Please note, however, the power of arrest applies only where the person *has* failed to attend the police station at the appointed time; it does not extend to situations where there is merely a 'reasonable suspicion' that the person has failed to attend and therefore both answers A and B are incorrect.

Question 13

Answer **D** — Section 7(3) of the Bail Act 1976 states:

> A person who has been released on bail in criminal proceedings and is under a duty to surrender into the custody of a court may be arrested without warrant by a constable—
> (a)   if the constable has reasonable grounds for believing that that person is not likely to surrender to custody.

Following arrest under s. 7(3), the person arrested must be brought before a magistrate as soon as practicable and, in any event, within

24 hours (s. 7(4)). Note that the section clearly states brought before a magistrate (justice) *not* just merely brought to the court precincts and therefore answers A and B are incorrect. This requirement is absolute and since the justice's jurisdiction under s. 7(5) to remand a detainee in custody only arises once s. 7(4) has been complied with, a detainee who is brought before the justice out of time cannot be remanded in custody (*R* v *Governor of Glen Parva Young Offenders Institution, ex parte G (a minor)* [1998] QB 887). The 24 hours is calculated from the time of arrest and not the time detention was authorised and therefore answer C is incorrect.

Question 14

Answer **C** — This area is dealt with by s. 1(1) of the Bail (Amendment) Act 1993, which states:

> Where a magistrates' court grants bail to a person who is charged with or convicted of—
>
> (a)   an offence punishable by a term of imprisonment of 5 years or more, or
>
> (b)   an offence under section 12 (taking a conveyance without authority) or 12A (aggravated vehicle taking) of the Theft Act 1968, the prosecution may appeal to a judge of the Crown Court against the granting of bail.

As s. 12 of the Theft Act 1968 is specifically mentioned in this section, answer B is incorrect. Further, s. 1(3) of the 1993 Act states:

> Such an appeal may be made only if—
>
> (a)   the prosecution made representations that bail should not be granted; and
>
> (b)   the representations were made before it was granted.

Therefore answer D is incorrect.

The only other factors to consider in the fact pattern are that of bail following the notice of appeal, and the time limit. To deal with the latter first, in *R* v *Middlesex Guildhall Crown Court, ex parte Okoli, The Times*, 2 August 2000, it was held that the 48 hours' period was from the date and not the time the oral notice was given and therefore answer A is incorrect. The question of bail is dealt with by s. 1(6) of the Bail (Amendment) Act 1993 which states:

> Upon receipt from the prosecution of oral notice of appeal from its decision to grant bail the magistrates' court shall remand in

custody the person concerned, until the appeal is determined or otherwise disposed of.

For this reason answer B is also incorrect. However, this does not override the fact that no appeal can be made as no representations were made before bail was granted.

Question 15

Answer **A** — The European Court and Commission have identified four grounds where the refusal of bail may be justified under the European Convention on Human Rights:

- fear of absconding;
- interference with the course of justice;
- the prevention of crime;
- the preservation of public order.

In relation to fear of absconding, the seriousness of the offence alone has been deemed not to be a sufficient reason to suppose a person will necessarily abscond (*Yagci and Sargin* v *Turkey* (1995) 20 EHRR 505) and answer B is therefore incorrect. In considering the prevention of crime, the European Court has held that, where the offender's previous convictions were not comparable either in nature or seriousness with the offence(s) charged, their use as grounds for refusing bail would not be acceptable for the purposes of Article 5 of the Convention (*Clooth* v *Belgium* (1991) 14 EHRR 717) and answer C is therefore incorrect. The temporary detention of a person where the particular gravity of the offence(s) and the likely public reaction is that the release may give rise to public disorder was considered in *Letellier* v *France* (1991) 14 EHRR 83 in relation to the preservation of public order. This was held to be a sound reason for remanding in custody and answer D is therefore incorrect. In *Ringeisen* v *Austria* (1971) 1 EHRR 455, interference with the course of justice was considered. If the detained person has previously been bailed and there was no evidence of interference with the course of justice, remanding in custody to prevent interference with the course of justice would be very difficult to justify.

3 COURT PROCEDURE AND WITNESSES

STUDY PREPARATION

This is what the whole process is all about. Although logically this chapter should appear at the end of the book, it makes practical sense to consider its contents here. The mechanics of getting evidence before a court largely come from statute and, as you would expect, contain a fair amount of detail.

It is important to understand who can give what evidence and under what circumstances; it is also important to know some of the more general restrictions that are placed on witnesses' evidence-in-chief and cross-examination.

QUESTIONS

Question 1

Where an accused has failed to appear at court, the court may proceed in his or her absence or may issue a warrant for his or her arrest. In determining whether an arrest warrant should be issued, the court has to consider the time between the service of the original summons and the date of the court appearance where the accused failed to appear. This time has to be 'a reasonable time'.

Which of the following time periods has been held to be 'reasonable'?

[A]   The summons can have been served the day before the trial.
[B]   The summons must have been served seven clear days prior to the trial.
[C]   The summons must have been served 14 clear days prior to the trial.
[D]   The summons must have been served 21 clear days prior to the trial.

Question 2

Children below a certain age are not permitted to be present in court during another person's trial unless they are a witness.

At what age does this restriction end?

[A]   14 years of age.
[B]   15 years of age.
[C]   16 years of age.
[D]   17 years of age.

Question 3

SAWYER, who is a youth, has been arrested for an offence of burglary, but denies the offence. He is released on police bail for further enquiries to be made, and returns one week later when he is charged with the offence.

Within what period must SAWYER first appear in court?

[A]   29 days from the day of his arrest.
[B]   29 days from the day he was charged.
[C]   36 days from the day of his arrest.
[D]   36 days from the day he was charged.

Question 4

YAU has been jointly charged with BELTON, with an offence of blackmail and both face trial as co-accused. The prosecution wishes to use YAU as a witness against BELTON, as YAU has indicated that BELTON was the main protagonist. This is supported by independent evidence.

In what circumstances can YAU give evidence against BELTON?

[A]   Only if YAU promises to plead guilty to the offence at a later date, after BELTON's trial.
[B]   If YAU pleads guilty on the day of the trial.
[C]   YAU can give evidence with no restrictions.
[D]   If the prosecutor tells YAU he will not be prosecuted.

Question 5

PROUD has been charged with an offence of theft, and her husband is a potential witness to the incident. PROUD'S solicitor wishes to call PROUD'S husband to give evidence on her behalf.

In relation to PROUD'S husband, which of the following is true?

[A]   He is a competent witness but not compellable.
[B]   He is a competent witness and is compellable.
[C]   He is not a competent witness and is not compellable.
[D]   He is not a competent witness but is compellable.

Question 6

BURGIN is appearing in court on a charge of unlawful sexual intercourse with a girl under 13. The victim has been called to give evidence and the defence question whether she is the age that she claims to be.

What evidence can be given to show the girl's age?

[A] Evidence of her parent that she is that age.
[B] Evidence of her birth certificate will suffice.
[C] Evidence of her birth certificate, supported by proof of identity.
[D] Any evidence of identity will suffice.

Question 7

ELDER is 17 years old and a witness to an offence of kidnapping. She is to be called to the Crown Court to give evidence for the prosecution, but ELDER has been receiving threats from the accused's family and they have yet to be dealt with for this intimidation. To avoid the accused's family attending and intimidating the witness, the prosecution seeks 'a special measures direction' to have ELDER's evidence given in private.

Who, if anyone, can the court exclude under this 'special measures direction'?

[A] Any person, including the accused but not his or her legal representatives.
[B] Any person except the accused and his or her legal representatives.
[C] The public only, the press would be allowed to stay as would the accused and his or her legal representatives.
[D] In this case the special measures direction may not be given as it is not a sexual offence.

Question 8

Constable WHALE and Constable CREASEY are witnesses in a case of theft. Both officers made pocket notebook entries regarding the incident, and have refreshed their memory from those notebooks prior to giving evidence. Constable WHALE also reminded Constable CREASEY, outside the court, of the index number of the vehicle involved. Neither officer refers to their pocket notebook whilst giving their evidence-in-chief.

In relation to refreshing memory, which of the following statements is true?

[A] Police officers can collaborate on the evidence they intend to give provided they record having done so.
[B] The prosecution must inform the defence that the officers have refreshed their memory from their notebooks.
[C] Defence counsel can inspect the officers' notebooks during cross-examination.
[D] Police officers should rely on their original notebooks only and they cannot use a copy of the notes.

Question 9

GRIGG is a witness in a Crown Court trial. Having received several silent phone calls which she perceived to be threatening, she is too frightened to give evidence. Constable MURTAGH who is investigating the offence believes GRIGG has a real fear of giving evidence.

Under s. 23 of the Criminal Justice Act 1988, which of the following is true in relation to GRIGG's statement being read out in place of her evidence-in-chief?

[A] GRIGG's statement can be read out provided it contains evidence relating to her fear.
[B] Constable MURTAGH must attend court and give sworn evidence of GRIGG's fear before the statement can be read out.
[C] GRIGG's statement cannot be read out as she has not received a direct threat or intimidation.
[D] GRIGG must attend court and give sworn evidence of her fear before the statement can be read out.

Question 10

HORWOOD is a newly-qualified prosecuting barrister engaged in an examination-in-chief of a witness. She asks the witness a leading question and the witness answers it, providing significant evidence of a fact in issue that directly incriminates the accused.

In relation to the consequence of asking the witness a leading question in this way, which of the following statements is true?

[A] The evidence obtained should be ruled inadmissible.
[B] The weight of the evidence obtained may be substantially reduced.
[C] The evidence obtained is admissible with no qualification.
[D] The leading question asked in this way would nullify proceedings.

Question 11

SOUTHWELL is standing trial at Crown Court for an offence of rape. His defence is based on consent and SOUTHWELL wishes to cross-examine the victim on her previous sexual behaviour, with the leave of the court.

In relation to this, which of the following statements is correct?

[A] Neither SOUTHWELL nor his legal representative can ask questions about the victim's previous sexual behaviour.
[B] SOUTHWELL can ask such questions, provided they relate to behaviour at or about the same time as the incident charged.
[C] SOUTHWELL's legal representative can ask questions about the victim's previous sexual behaviour.
[D] SOUTHWELL's legal representative can ask such questions provided they relate to behaviour at or about the same time as the incident in question.

Question 12

MILLIKEN is standing trial on a charge of violent disorder, which occurred during a large-scale public disorder situation. The prosecution relied heavily on the evidence of several police officers, some of whom gave evidence that they had seen the accused committing the offence. The officers were cross-examined only in relation to the evidence they had given. MILLIKEN whilst giving evidence, accused certain police officers of a conspiracy to fabricate the evidence against him. This was the first time the prosecution had been made aware of the defence's intention to raise this as an issue. The prosecutor wishes to recall the officers to rebut the accusation.

At this stage in the trial, having closed their case, will the prosecution be allowed to call evidence?

[A] Yes, but only if the defence accepts that there was a misunderstanding between counsel.
[B] Yes, as they could not reasonably have anticipated this defence.
[C] No, because this issue was not raised in cross-examination.
[D] No, because the prosecution must call the whole of their defence before closing their case — no exceptions.

ANSWERS

Question 1

Answer **A** — In the event of the non-appearance of the defendant, where he or she has not answered to bail, the court can issue a warrant for his or her arrest under s. 7 of the Bail Act 1976 or s. 1 of the Magistrates' Courts Act 1980. Section (1)(b) of the 1980 Act states the justice may:

> issue a warrant to arrest that person and bring him before a magistrates' court for the area or such magistrates' court as is provided . . .

However, if the accused fails to appear for the trial or adjourned trial of an information, a warrant for his or her arrest can still be issued, but this is reliant on when the summons was actually served on the accused. Section 13 of the 1980 Act outlines the criteria to be met to allow such a warrant to be issued, it states:

> (1)   Subject to the provisions of this section, where the court, instead of proceeding in the absence of the accused, adjourns or further adjourns the trial, the court may issue a warrant for his arrest.
> (2)   Where a summons has been issued, the court shall not issue a warrant under this section unless the condition in subsection (2A) below or that in subsection (2B) below is fulfilled.
> (2A)   The condition in this subsection is that it is proved to the satisfaction of the court, on oath or in such other manner as may be prescribed, that the summons was served on the accused within what appears to the court to be a reasonable time before the trial or adjourned trial.
> (2B)   The condition in this subsection is that—
> (a)   the adjournment now being made is a second or subsequent adjournment of the trial,
> (b)   the accused was present on the last (or only) occasion when the trial was adjourned, and
> (c)   on that occasion the court determined the time for the hearing at which the adjournment is now being made.

'A reasonable time before the trial' should be judged by the justices but it has been held that a summons to appear the following day was in order, and no statutory guidance is given as to a minimum period before the trial during which the summons must have been served and answers B, C and D are therefore incorrect.

Question 2

Answer **A** — There is extremely limited power at common law for a court to sit *in camera* (where the public are excluded) but this is supplemented by certain statutory provisions. One of these is that no child (i.e. a person *under* the age of 14) is permitted to be in court while criminal proceedings are in progress against a person other than the child themselves except where the child's presence is required as a witness or 'otherwise for the purposes of justice' (s. 36 of the Children and Young Persons Act 1933). So the restriction will be lifted when the child turns 14 years of age and answers B, C and D are therefore incorrect.

Question 3

Answer **C** — The Prosecution of Offences (Youth Court Time Limits) Regulations 1999 (SI 1999 No. 2743) provide for maximum time periods in relation to the three stages of proceedings in youth courts. They are 99 days from first court appearance to trial, 29 days from conviction to sentencing (answers A and B are therefore incorrect) and 36 days for the first court appearance from the date of arrest (answer D is therefore incorrect).

Question 4

Answer **B** — A co-accused may only give evidence for the prosecution if he or she has ceased to be a co-accused and answer C is therefore incorrect. A person would cease to be a co-accused when:

- The person pleads guilty, either on arraignment or during the course of the trial.
- The person is tried separately and convicted (although not mentioned in the *Evidence & Procedure Manual* this would include when he or she was acquitted (*R* v *Rowland* [1826] Ry & M 401)).
- The prosecution enters a *nolle prosequi*, putting to an end the proceedings against the person.

In all of these cases, a former co-accused becomes both competent and compellable for the prosecution.

So the accused must have pleaded guilty either before or during the trial and answer A is incorrect. Although a *nolle prosequi* is a 'promise not to prosecute', it must have been entered as such in the court records and it would not suffice that the accused had been promised he will not be prosecuted and answer D is incorrect, although there would almost certainly be a breach of process here.

Question 5

Answer **B** — As far as competence and compellability is concerned the law distinguishes between witnesses for the prosecution and witnesses for the defence. Here, the witness is one for the defence, and the law says that the spouse of the accused is competent to give evidence for the accused (s. 80(1)(b) of the Police and Criminal Evidence Act 1984). This remains the case even if they are jointly charged with an offence. Subject to one exception only, the spouse is also compellable to give evidence for the accused (s. 80(2)). The exception is where the spouses are jointly charged with an offence (s. 80(4)). Consequently, when giving evidence on behalf of the defence, a spouse will always be competent and therefore answers C and D are therefore incorrect. The husband is also compellable, as he is not jointly charged with the offence and answer A is therefore incorrect.

Question 6

Answer **C** — Issues surrounding age are dealt with by s. 9 of the Family Law Reform Act 1969, which states:

> The time at which a person attains a particular age expressed in years shall be the commencement of the relevant anniversary of the date of his birth.

This requires proof of date of birth not just identity and answer D is therefore incorrect. A birth certificate is usually accepted as evidence of age but if a certificate of birth is produced to prove age, evidence must also be adduced to positively identify the person as the person named in the certificate (*R* v *Rogers* (1914) 10 Cr App R 276) and answer B is therefore incorrect. The oral testimony of a member of the family will not suffice, although if the parent was present at the birth that evidence together with the certificate of birth may suffice — answer A is therefore incorrect.

Question 7

Answer **B** — Section 25(1) of the Youth Justice and Criminal Evidence Act 1999 states that 'a special measures direction' may provide for the exclusion of *any* persons from the court whilst the witness is giving evidence and answer C is therefore incorrect. This does not include the exclusion of the accused, legal representatives and any interpreter acting for the witness (s. 25(2)) and answer A is therefore incorrect. This direction may be used only where the proceedings relate to a sexual offence *or* there are reasonable grounds to believe that the witness has or will be intimidated by any person other than the accused — answer D is therefore incorrect.

Question 8

Answer **C** — It was held in *R v Bass* [1953] 1 All ER 1064 that two witnesses who have acted together can refresh their memories from notes made in collaboration, and a record should be made of that fact. This making of notes in collaboration does not extend to collaborating on their evidence outside the court prior to giving evidence. In *R v Skinner* (1994) 99 Cr App R 212, it was determined that, in refreshing their memory, witnesses should not discuss their evidence with other witnesses and answer A is therefore incorrect. There is no duty on the prosecution to inform the defence that any witness has refreshed their memory from an original note/statement (*Worley v Bentley* [1976] 2 All ER 449) and answer B is therefore incorrect. It is natural that, given the passing of time, witnesses may need to refresh their memory regarding the incident in question. In *R v Cheng* [1976] Crim LR 379, it was held that a copy or extract of the original notes etc. can be used in court to refresh the witness's memory if once the witness's memory has been refreshed he or she can swear positively to the facts and answer D is therefore incorrect. The courts have held that the giving of evidence is about reliability and not a test of memory (*R v Richardson* [1971] 2 QB 484; and *Lau Pak Ngam v R* [1966] Crim LR 443). However, where a police officer had refreshed his memory from his notebook outside the court, but had not used it in the witness box, it was held that the accused (or his or her legal representative) was entitled to examine the contents of the notebook and cross-examine the officer upon the relevant matters contained in it (*Owen v Edwards* (1983) 77 Cr App R 191).

Question 9

Answer **B** — Section 23 of the Criminal Justice Act 1988 allows witness statements to be read out where the witness 'does not give oral evidence through fear'. 'Fear' has been, through decided cases, given some definition. It has been held that where the court is certain that the witness is in fear as a result of the commission of the offence or of something said or done afterwards in relation to that offence, then s. 23 would be applicable (*R v Acton Justices, ex parte McMullen*

(1990) 92 Cr App Rep 98). Even this broad interpretation was further widened in *R v Martin* [1996] Crim LR 589 where it was held that no restriction should be imposed by the court as to what form or time this 'fear' should take. In *Martin*, a witness refused to give evidence, having been put in fear by the appearance of a silent stranger outside his door. There was no evidence of anything having been said or done by the stranger: the witness had simply interpreted the man's appearance as a threat (answer C is therefore incorrect). The only other requirement is that oral evidence of the fear must be given, for example, by a police officer. It cannot be proved by the written statement (*R v Belmarsh Magistrates' Court, ex parte Gilligan* [1998] 1 Cr App Rep 14) and answer A is therefore incorrect. Lastly, there is no requirement to cause the witness to attend at court and give evidence of her own fear; although unsworn evidence at the *voir dire* may be acceptable and answer D is therefore incorrect.

Question 10

Answer **B** — The general rule is that in examination-in-chief a witness may not be asked leading questions, i.e. questions framed in such a way as to suggest the answer sought or to take for granted the existence of facts yet to be established. Where leading questions are asked, these do not nullify proceedings and answer D is therefore incorrect, but the judge will stop an advocate asking questions in the prohibited form. Evidence obtained by such questions is not inadmissible and answer A is therefore incorrect, but the weight to be attached to it may be substantially reduced (*Moor v Moor* [1954] 1 WLR 927) and answer C is therefore incorrect.

Question 11

Answer **D** — Section 34 of the Youth Justice and Criminal Evidence Act 1999 states:

No person charged with a sexual offence may in any criminal proceedings cross-examine in person a witness who is the complainant . . .

This means that Southwell himself cannot cross-examine the victim about any matters and answer B is therefore incorrect. Should Southwell wish the complainant to be cross-examined, he must, or the court may, appoint a legal representative. Even when this is the case, there are restrictions on questions that can be asked of the victim. Section 41(1) states:

If at a trial a person is charged with a sexual offence, then, except with the leave of the court—
  (a)   no evidence may be adduced, and
  (b)   no question may be asked in cross-examination,
by or on behalf of the accused at the trial, about any sexual behaviour of the complainant.

'On behalf of' would include a legal representative, but there are exceptions, with leave of the court. Section 41(2) of the 1999 Act states:

The court may give leave only in relation to any evidence or question only on an application made by or on behalf of an accused, and may not give such leave unless it is satisfied— . . .

Section 41(3) states that:

  (3)   This subsection applies if the evidence or question relates to a relevant issue in the case and either—
  (a)   that the issue is not an issue of consent; or
  (b)   it is an issue of consent and the sexual behaviour of the complainant to which the evidence or question relates is alleged to have taken place at or about the same time as the event which is the subject matter of the charge against the accused;

So in the facts of the question, consent is in issue and counsel could ask questions, with leave of the court, provided they were about behaviour at or about the same time as the event which is the subject matter of the charge (answers A and C are therefore incorrect).

Question 12

Answer **B** — It is a general rule that all of the evidence which the prosecution intend to rely on should be called before the closure of their case (*R v Francis* [1991] 1 All ER 225). There are, however, some exceptions to this general rule and answer D is incorrect. The three recognised exceptions are:

- evidence not previously available;
- failure to call evidence by reason of inadvertence or oversight; and
- evidence in rebuttal of matters arising *ex improviso* (evidence which becomes relevant in circumstances which the prosecution could not have foreseen at the time when they presented their case).

In the facts outlined in the question, only the third exception arises. The principle of *ex improviso* deals with instances where during the case for the defence issues are raised that the prosecution could not have reasonably anticipated when they presented their case. In such instances the judge can allow the prosecution to call evidence in rebuttal of the defence put forward (*R* v *Pilcher* (1974) 60 Cr App R 1). This is true whether the issue is raised during cross-examination or in evidence-in-chief given by a defence witness and answer C is therefore incorrect. The judge also has discretion to admit evidence of a formal, technical or uncontentious nature, which, by reason of inadvertence or oversight, has not been adduced by the prosecution before the close of their case. In *R* v *Francis* the prosecution called an identification witness to give evidence that at a group identification he had identified the man standing in position number 20 but failed to call any evidence to prove that the man standing at that position was the appellant. The failure was due to a simple misunderstanding between counsel. The discretion of the judge to admit evidence after the close of the prosecution case is not limited to cases where an issue has arisen *ex improviso* or where what has been omitted is a mere formality and *Francis* was one of those rare cases falling outside the two established exceptions. Evidence can be adduced in circumstances where the defence do not accept there was a misunderstanding and answer A is therefore incorrect.

4 YOUTH JUSTICE AND YOUTH CRIME AND DISORDER

STUDY PREPARATION

Of all the areas covered by this subject, this one has probably seen the most changes over recent years. Youth justice is a central focus of the government's overall crime and disorder strategy and it is therefore a very important area for study.

The overall aims of the Crime and Disorder Act 1998 should be understood, along with the framework for youth justice that it introduced. Reprimands and warnings are important, as are parenting, child safety and curfew orders.

QUESTIONS

Question 1

In relation to the youth justice scheme under s. 37 of the Crime and Disorder Act 1998, what is its principal aim?

[A] To prevent offending by children and young persons.
[B] To prevent disorder by children and young persons.
[C] To establish a separate judicial process for children and young persons.
[D] To establish a local strategy to support children and young persons who are offenders.

Question 2

Under s. 39 of the Crime and Disorder Act 1998, the setting up of youth offending teams (acting in co-operation with others) is the responsibility of whom?

[A] The chief officer of police for a local area.
[B] The local authority for an area.
[C] The Youth Justice Board for an area.
[D] The youth offender panel for an area.

Question 3

LEAHY, who is a youth, pleaded guilty at Youth Court to a minor case of criminal damage. The court made a referral order to the youth offending team. A youth offender panel was formed and they are now considering making LEAHY pay for the cost of repair to the item he damaged.

Can the youth offender panel take this action?

[A] Yes, and this can be done without LEAHY's consent.
[B] Yes, provided LEAHY agrees to the proposed programme.
[C] No, a financial reparation cannot be ordered, but unpaid work can be considered.
[D] No, the only programme that can be considered is that of mediation.

Question 4

A Youth Justice Board is made up of members with extensive experience of the youth justice system. The members are appointed by the Secretary of State for a fixed period.

For how long is that fixed period?

[A] Five years maximum, with no re-appointments.
[B] Three years maximum, with no re-appointments.
[C] Five years, but the members can be re-appointed up to a maximum of ten years.
[D] Three years, but the members can be re-appointed up to a maximum of six years.

Question 5

In relation to reprimands and warnings provided by s. 65 of the Crime and Disorder Act 1998, which of the following statements is correct?

[A] The victim must consent before a reprimand or warning can be given.
[B] A reprimand can be given provided there is evidence to support a charge.
[C] A warning can be given where any previous warning was more than two years ago.
[D] Where the accused is 17 years of age, the reprimand/warning must be given in the presence of an appropriate adult.

Question 6

A parenting order can be imposed for compliance by the parent over a period not exceeding what length?

[A] 6 months.
[B] 12 months.
[C] 18 months.
[D] 24 months.

Question 7

A parenting order is being considered by the court in relation to BRIAN, who is 10 years of age and has been convicted of a theft, which took place on a Saturday. Part of this order would involve counselling sessions, and the child being escorted to school.

In relation to the proposed parenting order, which of the following statements is true?

[A] It cannot be made as such orders apply to a child under the age of 10 years only.
[B] It cannot include the child being escorted to school, as his offence was not committed on a school day.
[C] The magistrate should specify the amount of counselling needed.
[D] A member of the youth offending team should specify the amount of counselling needed.

Question 8

SHIELA is a particularly unruly 15 year old, in relation to whom the courts are considering a parenting order. Owing to her misbehaviour at home, SHIELA's uncle and aunt are currently looking after her, but they have no legal guardianship.

Can a parenting order be imposed on SHIELA's uncle and aunt?

[A] Yes, for the time being they are caring for SHIELA.
[B] Yes, provided the court's opinion is that they are caring for SHIELA.
[C] No, the order can be imposed on the biological parents only.
[D] No, as they do not have legal guardianship.

Question 9

ANDREW is 13 years old, and has been convicted of an offence at court. The court, however, is not satisfied that the making of a parenting order would be desirable in the interests of preventing the commission of any further offence by ANDREW.

In relation to the options the court may take regarding the parenting order, which of the following statements is true?

[A] The court must impose the order, as ANDREW is under 16 (a young person) and has been convicted of an offence.
[B] The court must impose the order as ANDREW is under 14 (a child) and has been convicted of an offence.
[C] The court need not impose the order, but must say in open court why it is not desirable.
[D] The court need not impose the order as it retains a discretion not to impose an order.

Question 10

In relation to a child safety order, which of the following persons/bodies are required to make the application to the magistrates' court under s. 11 of the Crime and Disorder Act 1998?

[A] The local authority.
[B] The chief officer of police.
[C] The Youth Justice Board.
[D] The youth offending team.

Question 11

A child can be placed under supervision for a permitted maximum period by the imposition of a child safety order. Unless there are exceptional circumstances, how long is that maximum period?

[A] 3 months.
[B] 6 months.
[C] 12 months.
[D] 15 months.

Question 12

The government has introduced child curfew schemes to tackle the problem of unsupervised young children (under 10) committing crime, anti-social activities and causing harm and misery to local communities. If such a scheme is imposed, during what specified times must the curfew take effect?

[A] 9 pm to 6 am.
[B] 9.30 am to 6.30 pm.
[C] 9 pm to 7 am.
[D] 10 pm to 7 am.

Question 13

Constable MAKINS is on patrol at 11.30 pm one night when she finds RICHARD, who is nine years old, in a public place. RICHARD is in breach of a child curfew scheme that has been imposed.

Which of the following statements is true in relation to Constable MAKINS?

[A] She must take the child to his home and should consider informing the local authority.
[B] She must take the child to his home and must inform the court who ordered the curfew.
[C] She may take the child to his home and must inform the local authority.
[D] She may take the child to his home and must inform the court who ordered the curfew.

ANSWERS

Question 1

Answer **A** — One of the functions of the Crime and Disorder Act 1998 is the prevention of disorder by all manner of people, not just children and young persons. There are specific sections which deal with disorder by children and young persons, but s. 37 is not one of those and answer B is therefore incorrect. Section 37(1) of Crime and Disorder Act 1998 states:

> It shall be the principal aim of the youth justice system to prevent offending by children and young persons.

Answers C and D are therefore incorrect.

Question 2

Answer **B** — Section 39 of Crime and Disorder Act 1998 states:

> . . . it shall be the duty of each local authority, acting in co-operation with the persons and bodies mentioned in subsection (3) below, to establish for their area one or more youth offending teams.

Those mentioned in subsection (3) are chief officers of police, probation board or health authority. Although acting in co-operation with others, the chief officer of police is not responsible for setting up a youth offending team and answer A is therefore incorrect. Youth offender panels are set up by a youth offending team and answer D is therefore incorrect. Youth Justice Boards are responsible for monitoring youth justice in a given area and answer C is therefore incorrect.

Question 3

Answer **B** — Sections 23 to 27 of the Powers of Criminal Courts (Sentencing) Act 2000 deal with youth offender contracts. This is a programme of behaviour to prevent re-offending, but it has to be agreed between the offender and the panel (s. 23(5)) and therefore answer A is incorrect. The terms of the programme may include a number of provisions; attendance at mediation sessions is one of them, but is by no means exclusive and answer D is therefore incorrect. The measures can include unpaid work or service, in addition to financial or other reparation to the victim and therefore answer C is incorrect.

Question 4

Answer **C** — Members of the Youth Justice Board are appointed by the Secretary of State for a fixed period of no longer than five years. They may be re-appointed, provided the total length of service does not exceed ten years (sch. 2, para. 2(5) of the Crime and Disorder Act 1998). Therefore answer C is the only correct response and answers A, B and D are incorrect.

Question 5

Answer **C** — Although a reprimand or warning under s. 65 of the Crime and Disorder Act 1998 requires the consent of the offender (s. 65(1)(c)), it does not require the consent of the victim, who effectively has no say in the course of action the police take and answer A is therefore incorrect (a decision not to prosecute is susceptible to judicial review however). The evidence available must do more than support a charge and must be at a level where there is a reasonable prospect of the child or young person being convicted of the offence and therefore answer B is incorrect. The presence of an appropriate adult is necessary only where the offender is *under* the age of 17 and answer D is therefore incorrect. Note a second warning is only available after a two-year gap. A second warning is available only once; if after another two-year gap the offender committed another offence, he or she would not qualify for a warning.

Question 6

Answer **B** — By s. 8 of the Crime and Disorder Act 1998 a parenting order lasts for a period not exceeding 12 months and answers A, C and D are therefore incorrect.

Question 7

Answer **D** — A parenting order can be imposed on a child or young person. For the purposes of the Crime and Disorder Act 1998, 'child' is someone under the age of 14 and 'young person' is someone of 14 years or over but under 18 (s. 117) and answer A is therefore incorrect. A parenting order is defined by s. 8(4)(a) as an order which requires the parent 'to comply, for a period not exceeding twelve months, with such requirements as are specified in the order'. The requirements provided by s. 8(4)(a) above are not specified but, in drafting the legislation certain examples were given. These included a parent escorting their child to school and a child being supervised by a responsible adult during the evenings (answer B is therefore incorrect). The counselling is defined in s. 8(4)(b) as 'to attend for a concurrent period not exceeding three months and not more than once in any week, such counselling and guidance sessions as may be specified in directions given by the responsible officer'. The responsible officer can be an officer of a local probation board, a social worker of a local authority social services department, a person nominated by a person appointed as chief education officer (under s. 532 of the Education Act 1996) and a member of a youth offending team and answer C is therefore incorrect.

Question 8

Answer **B** — Under s. 8(2) of the Crime and Disorder Act 1998, a parenting order may be made against:

- One or both biological parents (this could include an order against a father who may not be married to the mother).
- A person who is a guardian.

Therefore answer C is incorrect.

Guardians are defined as any person who, in the opinion of the court, has for the time being the care of a child or young person (s. 117(1)). It is not a matter of 'legal' guardianship, as the court will decide who is *in fact* a 'guardian' and therefore answer D is incorrect. For the same reason, answer A is also incorrect.

Question 9

Answer **C** — In relation to parenting orders the court will be required to establish whether or not the making of such an order is 'desirable' in the circumstances of a particular case. This is seen as an entirely subjective test and the court generally retains discretion not to impose an order. Section 9(1)(a) of the Crime and Disorder Act 1998, however, provides a statutory requirement in favour of making an order where the relevant condition relates to where a child or young person (under 16) is convicted of an offence therefore answer D is incorrect. If, however, the court is not satisfied that the 'relevant condition' is fulfilled (i.e. that the making of a parenting order would be desirable in the interests of preventing the commission of any further offence by the child or young person under 16), the court must state in open court that it is not so satisfied, and why it is not. There is then some limited discretion where s. 9(1)(a) applies and therefore answers A and B are incorrect.

Question 10

Answer **A** — Section 11 of the Crime and Disorder Act 1998 states:

(1) Subject to subsection (2) below, if a magistrates' court, on the application of a local authority, is satisfied that one or more of the conditions specified in subsection (3) below are fulfilled with respect to a child under the age of 10, it may make an order (a 'child safety order') . . .

The section provides evidence of the government's determination to deliver crime prevention through a partnership approach. A local authority with social services responsibilities must make the application for such an order. However, it would probably be the police who first become aware of the misconduct, which triggers such an application. It is, however, the local authority only who must make the application for such an order and answers B, C and D are therefore incorrect.

Question 11

Answer **A** — The permitted maximum period of supervision of a child safety order is three months. If the court is satisfied that the circumstances of the case are exceptional it can extend the order up to a maximum of 12 months (s. 11(4) of the Crime and Disorder Act 1998). Therefore answers B, C and D are incorrect.

Question 12

Answer **A** — Section 14(2)(a) of the Crime and Disorder Act 1998 states that a curfew will be 'during specified hours (between 9 pm and 6 am)'. Therefore answers B, C and D are incorrect.

Question 13

Answer **C** — Section 14 of the Crime and Disorder Act 1998 states that it is a local authority, in liaison with the Secretary of State (who needs to confirm it), that makes a child curfew scheme.

Therefore as the courts do not impose a curfew, they do not need to be informed of a breach and answers B and D are incorrect.

If there has been a contravention of a curfew notice, s. 15 of the 1998 Act states:

> (2) The constable shall, as soon as practicable, inform the local authority for the area that the child has contravened the ban.
> (3) The constable may remove the child to the child's place of residence unless he has reasonable cause to believe that the child would, if removed to that place, be likely to suffer significant harm.

Informing the local authority who imposed the scheme is mandatory, but taking the child home is not and therefore answer A is incorrect.

Section 15(3) does not state what a constable should do with a child if he or she does not remove the child to its home. However, it would seem appropriate to use the power under s. 46 of the Children Act 1989 in removing the child to suitable accommodation, i.e. a police station or care of social services.

5 PRIVILEGE AND PUBLIC POLICY

STUDY PREPARATION

A person's protection against self-incrimination was pretty strongly defended by the courts *before* the Human Rights Act 1998; now it is almost sacrosanct. Even the statutory exceptions to the rule will be carefully scrutinised against the general requirements of the European Convention and it is important to understand how and when these issues of self-incrimination arise.

Another important evidential area where the courts stand firm is that of legal professional privilege and you should know the extent of this privilege and where it will/will not apply.

Not every protection is aimed at the defendant and a very important procedural device for the police and prosecutors can be found in public interest immunity. Again, it is necessary to know the extent of this feature which is open to the prosecution to claim in any proceedings.

QUESTIONS

Question 1

HUDSON is a witness in a trial for theft and has been asked a question relating to the recovery of property subject to the charge. HUDSON realises that the answer to the question would incriminate him and his wife in an offence of handling stolen goods contrary to s. 22 of the Theft Act 1968, but not the original theft.

Can HUDSON refuse to answer the question, claiming privilege against self-incrimination?

[A]   Yes, HUDSON can claim privilege against self-incrimination for himself and his wife.
[B]   Yes, HUDSON can claim privilege against self-incrimination for himself but not his wife.
[C]   No, HUDSON must answer the question, but the answer cannot be used in evidence against him or his wife in any trial for handling stolen goods.
[D]   No, HUDSON must answer the question, and the answer can be used in evidence against him, but not against his wife, in any trial for handling stolen goods.

Question 2

JONES is giving sworn evidence in his own defence, in a trial where he stands accused of burglary. It is strongly suspected that he was involved in a series of burglaries with a similar *modus operandi* (MO) leading up to the one he is accused of. There is, however, no proof of his involvement in the other offences. Section 1 of the Criminal Evidence Act 1898 deals with defendants who give evidence from the witness box and the privilege of self-incrimination.

In relation to JONES being cross-examined about the burglaries with the same MO, which of the following statements is true?

[A] JONES can be asked questions about those matters and must answer as he is giving *sworn* evidence from the witness box.
[B] JONES can be asked questions about those matters and must answer as he is giving evidence from the witness box.
[C] JONES can be asked questions about those matters, but need not answer, with no inferences being drawn from that silence.
[D] JONES cannot be asked questions that tend to incriminate him if those questions relate to previous, unsubstantiated, suspicion of crime.

Question 3

COX is selling a house and draws up a contract that is, in essence, fraudulent. It contains details of planning permission that has in fact *not* been obtained, but has added £20,000 to the value of the house. COX has sent the contract to his solicitor seeking her advice, knowing with the contract approved by his solicitor he will be able to go ahead with his fraud. COX has several exchanges with his solicitor regarding the contract. COX'S solicitor, however, is not aware of the purpose for which her advice is sought. As yet no one else is aware of the fraud, and litigation is not contemplated.

Are the 'communications' between COX and his solicitor subject to legal privilege?

[A] Yes, all communications between client and legal adviser are privileged.

[B] Yes, even though the legal adviser is unaware of the purpose of the advice.

[C] No, as privilege applies to communications where litigation is contemplated only.

[D] No, as the communication is in furtherance of crime or fraud.

Question 4

BOLTON had been arrested for an offence of supplying a controlled drug, and had been advised, by his solicitor, to remain silent during police interviews as the solicitor believed BOLTON was suffering from withdrawal symptoms. BOLTON had been examined by the police surgeon and deemed fit for interview. At the conclusion of the interview, the solicitor said 'I advised my client to remain silent as he should not have been interviewed in his condition, despite what your doctor says'.

In relation to this legal advice, can the solicitor be called to give evidence in a future trial as to the advice he gave?

[A] No, a solicitor *must* always refuse to give oral evidence about advice that is legally privileged.
[B] No, BOLTON had not given a waiver at the time, and the solicitor *must* refuse to give oral evidence.
[C] Yes, as by explaining the reasons for the advice at the time privilege had been waived.
[D] Yes, but *only* if BOLTON waives his legal privilege at the trial.

Question 5

GOODRIDGE was charged with murder but the Crown Prosecution Service discontinued the case. GOODRIDGE took out a malicious prosecution case against the police, and his solicitors asked for certain documents to be made available to them. These documents related to reports and correspondence between the police and the Director of Public Prosecutions and also a report sent to the Police Complaints Authority. The Crown Prosecution Service do not want to hand over these police communications on the grounds of public interest immunity.

Which, if any, of the communications is likely to attract public interest immunity in these circumstances?

[A] None of the communications are likely to be granted public interest immunity.
[B] Only the reports to the Director of Public Prosecutions are likely to be granted public interest immunity.
[C] Only the reports to the Police Complaints Authority are likely to be granted public interest immunity.
[D] All the communications will attract public interest immunity.

Question 6

Constable SILLITOE made a grievance alleging sexual discrimination to her supervisory officer. The supervisory officer made some enquiries under the force grievance procedure and obtained statements from officers. As a result of the information contained in these statements there was a formal investigation relating to a criminal offence. Part of the investigation involved obtaining a search warrant to search a police officer's home. The investigating officer prepared a formal report, and a report was also sent to the Director of Public Prosecutions.

Which of these communications would *not* attract public interest immunity?

[A] The reports sent to the Director of Public Prosecutions.
[B] The statements made during the course of the grievance procedure.
[C] The document upon which the search warrant was obtained.
[D] The report prepared by the investigating officer.

Question 7

Whilst presiding over a case at Crown Court, His Honour Justice LANE witnesses the accused leap over the dock and assault a key prosecution witness. This results in serious injuries and a charge of assault against the accused.

Is the judge able to give evidence at the future trial for the assault?

[A] Yes, the judge is both competent and compellable to give evidence in this case.
[B] Yes, although not compellable he is competent and should be relied on not to allow his non-compellability to stand in the way of his giving evidence.
[C] No, a judge, although competent, cannot be compelled to give evidence for matters he witnesses as a judge.
[D] No, a judge is not a competent witness to give evidence for matters he witnesses as a judge.

ANSWERS

Question 1

Answer **C** — One of the fundamental rights in English and Welsh law is that of the principle of privilege against self-incrimination, which is almost absolute. Section 31 of the Theft Act is one of the statutory exceptions to the principle of privilege against self-incrimination. Hudson *must* answer the question and cannot claim privilege (answers A and B are therefore incorrect), but would be protected where the answer may incriminate him in any charge under the Theft Act 1968. Section 31 simply requires questions to be answered and orders to be complied with in proceedings for the recovery or administration of any property or dealing with property. Where such answers may incriminate the witness or his or her spouse and leave them liable to a charge for an offence under the 1968 Act, the answers may not be used in proceedings for any such offence. Even though the answers may not be used in proceedings for any such offence, they might be useful in pointing towards areas where evidence might be found linking the witness to the offence and answer D is therefore incorrect.

Article 6 of the European Convention on Human Rights could be used as a 'shield' against self-incrimination. In the Scottish case of *Jardine* v *Crowe* 1999 SLT 1023 the defendant refused to give details of the driver of his vehicle after a relevant offence when required to do so by the police under s. 172 of the Road Traffic Act 1988. He argued that the requirement infringed Article 6 on the grounds that it forced him to incriminate himself. This argument was disposed of in the English and Welsh courts in *DPP* v *Wilson, The Times*, 21 March 2001. The Queen's Bench Divisional Court held that the use in evidence of a defendant's compulsory admission under the Road Traffic Act 1988 that he was the driver of a vehicle at the time when a road traffic offence was committed did not infringe his privilege against self-incrimination or right to a fair trial under Article 6. The issues raised by s. 31 are, however, arguably very different.

Question 2

Answer **D** — Since 1898 the accused has been a competent witness in his or her own defence. Section 1(2) and (3) of the Criminal Evidence Act 1898, as amended by the Youth Justice and Criminal Evidence Act 1999, together ensure that, when it comes to cross-examination, the accused is not treated in quite the same way as an ordinary witness. Section 1(2) removes the privilege against self-incrimination which the accused would otherwise enjoy in respect of the offence with which he is charged. Section 1(3) provides a protection (or shield as it is often called) against cross-examination in relation to various aspects of the past misconduct of the accused (*Jones* v *DPP* [1962] AC 635). In *Jones*, their Lordships held that s. 1(3) gives the accused person a 'shield'. The accused 'shall not be asked' certain questions unless certain conditions apply. That 'shield' is defined in the Act in s. 1(3)(i) as 'proof that he has committed or been convicted of such other offence is admissible evidence to show that he is guilty of an offence with which he is then charged'. In the circumstances of the question, there is no proof that Jones committed the similar burglaries and so he would be offered the protection of the 'shield' of s. 1(3). Answers A, B and C are therefore incorrect.

Question 3

Answer **D** — Legal privilege can be defined as attaching to communications between the client and his or her legal adviser made for the purpose of enabling the client to obtain (or the adviser to give) legal advice about any matter, whether or not litigation was contemplated at the time. Answer C is therefore incorrect. There are, however, exceptions to legal privilege and answer A is therefore incorrect. Communications in furtherance of crime or fraud are a well-recognised exception to the principle of legal privilege (*R* v *Derby Magistrates' Court, ex parte B* [1996] AC 487). In *R* v *Cox* (1884) 14 QBD 153, a solicitor was compelled to disclose communications with the accused, in which the accused had sought his advice in drawing up a bill of sale alleged to be fraudulent. In *Derby* it was held that if a client applies to a legal adviser for advice intended to facilitate or to guide the client in the commission of a crime and the legal adviser is ignorant of the purpose for which his advice is sought, the communication between the two is not privileged (answer B is therefore incorrect).

Question 4

Answer **C** — Naturally any advice in relation to a police interview would be subject to legal privilege. Privilege belongs to the client and he or she can waive it and answer A is therefore incorrect. So if Bolton did waive his right at the trial, the solicitor could be called, but answer D says 'only', indicating that this is the only way in which privilege can be waived, and this is not true. If the defence reveal the basis or reason for the solicitor's advice to the accused not to answer police questions, this will amount to a waiver of privilege whether the revelation is made by the accused or by the solicitor acting on behalf of the accused (answer B is therefore incorrect), and whether the revelation is made in the course of pre-trial questioning or at court (*R* v *Bowden* [1999] 1 WLR 823).

Question 5

Answer **A** — Public interest immunity can be applied for anything and it is a matter of discretion for the courts. There are some examples, however, which give guidance. In *Goodridge* v *Chief Constable of Hampshire* [1999] 1 All ER 896, a malicious prosecution case brought by a person charged with murder where the case was later discontinued, it was held that reports and correspondence passing between the police and the Director of Public Prosecutions and a report sent to the Police Complaints Authority were not subject to public interest immunity and therefore answers B, C and D are incorrect.

Question 6

Answer **B** — Public interest immunity generally attaches to police communications, which would include documents upon which the search warrant was obtained, reports sent to the Director of Public Prosecutions and reports prepared by the investigating officers involved in complaints against police. Answers A, C and D are therefore incorrect. Public interest immunity does not generally attach to statements made during the course of a police grievance procedure, initiated by an officer, alleging either racial or sexual discrimination (*Commissioner of Police of the Metropolis* v *Locker* [1993] 3 All ER 584).

Question 7

Answer **A** — A judge cannot be compelled to give evidence of matters of which he became aware relating to, and as a result of, the *performance of his judicial functions* (as opposed to unconnected matters, such as a crime committed in the face of the court). However, the judge remains competent to give evidence, and if a situation arises where his evidence is vital, the judge should be able to be relied on not to allow his non-compellability to stand in the way of his giving evidence (*Warren* v *Warren* [1997] QB 488). So the difference is in whether the judge is simply a witness to an offence or aware of matters because he or she was the judge. Here the judge is a witness and as such is a normal competent and compellable witness and answers B, C and D are therefore incorrect. Had the judge become aware of matters because he or she was the judge, answer D would have been the correct response.

6 EVIDENCE

STUDY PREPARATION

The subject matter covered in this chapter is at the heart of the whole area of evidence and procedure. As with chapter 3, most of the chapter is concerned with the fundamentals — what type of evidence can be given by whom to show what. There is a fair amount of complex law in this part and unfortunately it has to be separated and assimilated.

It is critical to understand the issues of weight and admissibility. It is also critical to understand the different standards of proof, civil and criminal — the latter because it is the only way in which you can prove any criminal liability and the former because it is relevant to issues that the defendant may have to prove. The standard of proof is different from the burden of proof (although they are closely linked) and again it is important to know where the relevant burden lies.

Documentary evidence is increasingly relied upon in criminal trials and this area needs attention.

A further area of great practical importance is the legislation that sets out when adverse inferences can be drawn from silences or failure by the defendant to mention certain things. These are often confused, with some officers getting the various components mixed up.

QUESTIONS

Question 1

Watkins is appearing in court on two indictments.

1. Theft.
2. Handling stolen goods.

His defence to count 2 is that he did not know that the goods were stolen. Can the prosecution adduce evidence of a conviction of theft that WATKINS had two years ago?

[A] Yes, provided seven days' notice of the intention to do so was given.
[B] Yes, this is a presumption of fact and is admissible.
[C] No, evidence of bad character may never be given prior to conviction.
[D] No, in the circumstances of this case, the evidence will not be allowed.

Question 2

Which of the following statements most accurately describes the 'best evidence rule'?

[A] Oral evidence given by a witness in court.
[B] An original document.
[C] Any documentary evidence.
[D] Evidence that goes to prove a case.

Question 3

In presenting a prosecution case where the defendant has pleaded not guilty, certain facts always have to be proved. Which of the following are amongst those facts?

1. The identity of the accused.
2. The nature of the act.
3. The existence of the necessary knowledge or intent.

[A] Facts 2 and 3 only.
[B] All three facts.
[C] Facts 1 and 3 only.
[D] Facts 1 and 2 only.

Question 4

Detective Constable GARDNER has been investigating a complicated fraud. A large amount of evidence has been obtained, all of which is admissible. Detective Constable GARDNER has, however, heard that the judge can exclude evidence, even though it is admissible.

In relation to this, which of the following statements is true?

[A] The trial judge always has the discretion to exclude any evidence tendered by the prosecution.
[B] The trial judge has discretion to exclude evidence, but only when so requested by the defence.
[C] The trial judge has discretion to exclude evidence only where s. 78 of the Police and Criminal Evidence Act 1984 has been clearly breached.
[D] The trial judge has no discretion to exclude legally admissible evidence.

Question 5

PREECE has been arrested for an offence of burglary and requests PARSONS, a solicitor, to advise him. PARSONS advises PREECE not to answer questions during the interview, and PREECE takes this advice. During PREECE's trial, the prosecution alleges that the defence have manufactured a story that is not true since the interview, and asks for inferences to be drawn from the silence during the interview.

What evidence can PREECE adduce to counter this submission?

[A] He may call his solicitor to give evidence to rebut this allegation, and the solicitor must give evidence.

[B] He may give evidence to rebut this allegation, but may not call his solicitor.

[C] He may not give evidence to rebut this allegation, but his solicitor can give such evidence if he or she agrees to do so.

[D] No evidence can be given to rebut this allegation as the advice is covered by legal privilege.

Question 6

ASQUITH is on trial for an offence of rape, and has been sworn to give evidence. Prosecuting counsel asks him, 'It is true is it not, that you did have sexual intercourse with Miss DAVIES, and at that time you clearly knew that she did not consent?'

ASQUITH remains silent, and refuses to answer the question.

Will the jury be entitled to draw any inferences from ASQUITH's refusal to answer this question?

[A] No, ASQUITH has a right not to incriminate himself and inferences may not be drawn.

[B] No, the prosecution has no right to ask such questions, and inferences may not be drawn.

[C] Yes, ASQUITH has refused without good cause to answer the question, and inferences may be drawn.

[D] Yes, and the inferences drawn from this refusal would be enough to convict.

Question 7

Constable NICHOLS is giving evidence at the trial of BRIDGES, who is charged with a drink driving offence. Constable NICHOLS has been asked to explain the workings of the breath test device, which she does. She is then asked to produce the device, as real evidence, to the court for inspection.

In relation to Constable NICHOLS, which of the following statements is correct?

[A] She must produce the actual device used to carry out the test or her oral evidence may be adversely affected.

[B] Failure to produce the actual device used will adversely affect the evidence obtained on the machine.

[C] She may produce a similar device, as there is no requirement to produce the actual device used.

[D] Failure to produce the actual or a similar device will have no adverse affect on her oral evidence.

Question 8

JOHNSON, a well-known criminal with a history of violent offences, has just been shot by a rival. Constable KHALID is the first officer at the scene. She speaks to JOHNSON and he says, 'I am dying, I know I am, before I go I want to tell you that it was me and FORD who did those armed robberies last year'. Shortly after this JOHNSON dies.

If FORD is charged with the robberies, can Constable KHALID give this hearsay evidence in court?

[A] Yes, using the 'dying declaration' exception to hearsay.

[B] No, it is not admissible as it is hearsay and none of the 'exceptions' apply.

[C] Yes, using the 'res gestae' exception to hearsay.

[D] Yes, using the 'statements made by deceased' exception to hearsay.

Question 9

CALLARD has been summonsed for an offence of failing to conform to a red light at automatic traffic signals. Her defence is that the traffic signals were not working properly at the time she allegedly drove through the red light.

Which of the following statements is true?

[A] The prosecution must prove beyond all reasonable doubt that the lights were working correctly.
[B] The defence must prove beyond all reasonable doubt that the lights were *not* working correctly.
[C] The prosecution must prove on the balance of probabilities that the lights were working correctly.
[D] The defence must prove on the balance of probabilities that the lights were *not* working correctly.

Question 10

Doctor LANFORD has been charged with two, separate, indecent assaults on female patients, where he touched their breasts in an indecent and unwanted manner. One patient was receiving a vaginal examination; the other had an in-growing toenail. Both women state that the doctor used unusual and offensive language during the assaults. The doctor admits he carried out the medical examinations, but denies indecently assaulting either patient.

Will the evidence of each patient be admitted to corroborate the allegation of the other?

[A] No, as neither patient witnessed the other's incident.
[B] No, as the reasons for their medical examinations differed.
[C] Yes, the evidence is likely to be admitted as similar fact evidence.
[D] Yes, it is not hearsay and any oral statement made by the accused is admissible as evidence.

Question 11

HYDE was the victim of a serious sexual assault and she is alleging that WILSON raped her. There are no witnesses to the incident and no physical evidence. There is, however, substantial circumstantial evidence. WILSON has denied being the perpetrator, but has been charged and will appear at the Crown Court.

In relation to corroboration, which of the following statements is true?

[A] In this case corroboration is required in law.
[B] Although corroboration is not required, the judge must give a corroboration warning to the jury.
[C] In this case corroboration is not required at all.
[D] Although corroboration is not required, the judge may choose to give a corroboration warning to the jury.

Question 12

PHILLIPS is a paedophile who commits homosexual acts with young boys. Following a complaint from one boy PHILLIPS is arrested and charged. His *modus operandi* is to sit the boys on the floor and then dance round them wearing a doctor's white coat and carrying a stethoscope, prior to requiring the boys to perform oral sex on him. The investigation reveals that there are five other victims, who were assaulted in this way, but no charges were made.

Can the five boys give evidence of what happened to them at the trial for the offence PHILLIPS is now charged with?

[A] No, it is evidence of bad character and would not be allowed.
[B] No, because PHILLIPS was never charged in relation to those boys.
[C] Yes, as the striking similarity rule applies.
[D] Yes, the evidence of the five boys is corroboration that the offence charged took place.

Question 13

BURNS is charged with an offence of murder. The circumstances are that he allowed a man, GREY, whom he had met in a nightclub to stay at his house. At some point a fight took place and GREY was fatally stabbed by BURNS. In his defence, BURNS has given sworn evidence that he stabbed GREY as a last resort to fight off his continued sexual advances. BURNS adduces evidence that he finds homosexuality repugnant. To rebut this, the prosecution wish to introduce BURNS's previous convictions; one for buggery with a man, and two for gross indecency in men's public toilets.

Is the judge likely to allow this evidence to be adduced?

[A] No, the previous convictions have nothing in common with the offence charged.
[B] Yes, this is similar fact evidence and is likely to be allowed.
[C] No, a person's previous convictions may not be put before a court until the case has been proved.
[D] Yes, as a sworn witness BURNS loses his right not to have his previous convictions introduced.

Question 14

CHILDS has been charged with conspiracy to defraud, and an investigation is in progress. The fraud squad has discovered that CHILDS used to send pager messages to a contact in Switzerland. This was done by contacting the Pager Company, who wrote down the message on a pad and then transmitted it electronically. Some of these messages show CHILDS was involved in fraud, however, the operator of the machine had no knowledge of whether the messages were true or not.

Is it likely that the written message pad could be tendered as evidence in a 'business document' under s. 24 of the Criminal Justice Act 1988?

[A] Yes, it fits the relevant criteria and would be admitted.
[B] No, the person who made the document has to know the truth of its contents.
[C] Yes, provided the witness was unavailable to attend court.
[D] No, as CHILDS is not the maker of the document it is inadmissible.

Question 15

Non-expert witnesses, in certain cases, can give evidence of opinion to the court. In relation to this which of the following statements, if either, is/are true?

1. *Only* police officers can give evidence that, in their opinion, a person is drunk by referring to facts on which the opinion is based.
2. *Any* competent witness can give evidence that, in their opinion, a person is drunk by referring to facts on which the opinion is based.

[**A**] Both statements.
[**B**] Neither statement.
[**C**] Statement 1 only.
[**D**] Statement 2 only.

Question 16

TURNER has been charged with an offence of forgery. He intends to call a handwriting expert to rebut the prosecution evidence at his trial at Crown Court.

Which of the following statements is true?

[**A**] The defence do not have to provide pre-trial disclosure to the prosecution on this matter.
[**B**] The defence must allow the prosecution to consider whether the witness is competent to give expert opinion.
[**C**] The defence must furnish the prosecution with a summary of the evidence the expert will give.
[**D**] The defence must furnish the prosecution with a statement, in writing, of the expert's finding.

Question 17

ROBBINS has been charged with an offence of perjury. Whilst giving evidence as a sworn witness in a rape case, she stated that she had become pregnant by the rape. Records show that she gave birth two weeks after the alleged attack.

Given that these records will be admissible, what else will the prosecution have to prove to show that she cannot have become pregnant at the time of the alleged rape?

[A] Expert witness testimony that human gestation lasts nine months.
[B] Testimony from any competent witness testimony that human gestation lasts nine months.
[C] No specific proof is required; it is common knowledge that human gestation lasts nine months.
[D] Expert witness testimony that human gestation lasts longer than two weeks.

Question 18

Evidence of good character of an accused may be relevant to which, if either, of the following situations?

1. The integrity of the defendant in relation to statements made by him to the police that he was free from blame.
2. Demonstrating that the accused has not behaved in the alleged manner before, and so may not have done so this time.

[A] Both situations.
[B] Situation 1 only.
[C] Situation 2 only.
[D] Neither situation.

Question 19

BUTLER stands charged with the rape of two women. In both cases, whilst being driven in BUTLER's car, the women were forced to take part in oral intercourse to the point of ejaculation. The women were then taken to a wooded area and raped. BUTLER's ex-girlfriend is willing to give evidence that, albeit by consent, she regularly performed oral intercourse in the car and then went to a wooded area and had sexual intercourse with him. BUTLER's defence is that of mistaken identity.

Is it likely that the ex-girlfriend will be allowed to give this evidence?

[A] No, as what took place with her was not an offence; it would not be allowed as similar fact evidence.
[B] No, this is evidence of bad character and would not be allowed even as similar fact evidence.
[C] Yes, this is *prima facie* circumstantial evidence tending to show guilt, and would be allowed.
[D] Yes, it is likely that this evidence will be allowed under the similar fact principle.

Question 20

DAWLISH has been accused of an assault by his neighbour, and has attended voluntarily at the police station. He is not arrested but is interviewed regarding the assault. During the interview, the police officer notices there are marks on DAWLISH's knuckles consistent with details of the assault allegation. The officer reasonably believes that the marks may be attributable to the accused's participation in the assault. The officer asks DAWLISH to account for the marks, and DAWLISH refuses to answer the question.

Can inferences be drawn from DAWLISH's refusal at court?

[A] Yes, provided the officer gave a 'special warning' before asking the question.
[B] Yes, he has failed to account for a mark which may be attributable to the crime charged.
[C] No, as he was not arrested for the offence.
[D] No, there is no evidence linking the mark to the assault.

ANSWERS

Question 1

Answer **D** — Section 27 of the Theft Act 1968, which deals with this issue, states:

> (3) Where a person is being proceeded against for handling stolen goods (but not for any offence other than handling stolen goods), then at any stage of the proceedings, if evidence has been given of his having or arranging to have in his possession the goods the subject of the charge, or of his undertaking or assisting in, or arranging to undertake or assist in, their retention, removal, disposal or realisation, the following evidence shall be admissible for the purpose of proving that he knew or believed the goods to be stolen goods—
>
>   (a)   evidence that he has had in his possession, or has undertaken or assisted in the retention, removal, disposal or realisation of, stolen goods from any theft taking place not earlier than 12 months before the offence charged; and
>
>   (b)   (provided that seven days' notice in writing has been given to him of the intention to prove the conviction) evidence that he has within the five years preceding the date of the offence charged been convicted of theft or of handling stolen goods.

This provision applies to all forms of handling (*R* v *Ball* [1983] 1 WLR 801), and can be used where handling is the *only* offence involved in the proceedings. Such evidence is, however, evidence of bad character and therefore answer C is incorrect. This is a presumption of fact and if the indictment had been 'handling' only, then provided that seven days' notice was given, it would have been admissible. However, for the reasons outlined here, answers A and B are incorrect.

Question 2

Answer **B** — The best evidence rule has lost its impact since it came into being in 1745, i.e. when evidence was written on parchment with quills! In 1989 Lloyd LJ in *R* v *Governor of Pentonville Prison, ex parte Osman* [1990] 1 WLR 277 said 'although the little loved best evidence rule has been dying for some time, recent authorities (cases) suggest that it is still not quite dead'.

In *Osman*, Lloyd LJ referred to *Kajala* v *Noble* (1982) 75 Cr App R 149 where Ackner LJ said:

The old rule, that a party must produce the best evidence that the nature of the case will allow, and that any less good evidence is to be excluded, has gone by the board long ago. The only remaining instance of it is that, if an original document is available in one's hands, one must produce it; that one cannot give secondary evidence by producing a copy.

Today the best evidence rule can best be described as original documentary evidence (therefore answer A is incorrect), and not merely any documentary evidence (therefore answer C is incorrect). Evidence adduced that goes to prove a case is too broad and could not be described as 'best evidence' (therefore answer D is incorrect).

Question 3

Answer **B** — Where the defendant has pleaded not guilty to the charge, the onus is on the prosecution to prove the whole of their case. This includes all of the acts listed (*R* v *Sims* [1946] KB 531) and answers A, C and D are therefore incorrect.

Question 4

Answer **A** — At common law the trial judge has a discretion to exclude any evidence if it is felt that its prejudicial effect outweighs its probative value and answer D is therefore incorrect. This is true even where the evidence is legally admissible; it is for the judge to ensure that the accused receives a fair trial (*R* v *Sang* [1980] AC 402). The judge can apply the discretion even where the defence make no formal submissions and answer B is therefore incorrect. Although s. 78 of the Police and Criminal Evidence Act 1984 allows evidence to be excluded, the judge's common law discretion goes beyond that particular section (e.g. hearsay evidence) and therefore answer C is incorrect.

Question 5

Answer **A** — Where a defendant says that advice was received from his or her solicitor not to answer questions, the accused is entitled to give evidence of the conversation with the solicitor prior to interview to rebut any allegation of post-interview fabrication and answer C is therefore incorrect. In *R* v *Daniel* it was also held that the defendant is entitled to call the solicitor to give evidence of the advice given before interview (*R* v *Daniel* (1998) 162 JP 578) and answer B is therefore incorrect. The fact the defendant calls the solicitor waives any legal privilege that may have existed and answer D is therefore incorrect. Of course, having given evidence-in-chief, the prosecution will be entitled to cross-examine the solicitor on that pre-interview conversation.

Question 6

Answer **C** — A jury may draw inferences where a defendant refuses, without good cause, to answer a question properly put. Once the defendant becomes a sworn witness he or she loses the privilege against self-incrimination and answer A is therefore incorrect. Also, the defendant may be asked questions that tend to incriminate them and answer B is therefore incorrect. So here inferences may be drawn. However, such inferences alone, without supporting evidence would not be sufficient to convict and answer D is therefore incorrect.

Question 7

Answer **C** — Real evidence usually takes the form of a material object for inspection by the court. This evidence is to prove, either that the material object in question exists, or to enable the court to draw an inference from its own observation as to the object's value and physical condition. It is normally accompanied by written testimony and identified by a witness. This testimony usually includes an explanation of the connection between the exhibit and the facts in issue or the relevance to an issue. Little, if any, weight can attach to real evidence in the absence of accompanying testimony identifying the object and connecting it with the facts in issue. There is no rule of law that an object must be produced, or its non-production excused, before oral evidence may be given about it. For example, it is not necessary for the police to produce the very breath test device used by them on a particular occasion (see *Castle* v *Cross* [1984] 1 WLR 1372) and answers A and B are therefore incorrect. However, the weight of the oral evidence may be adversely affected by the non-production of the object in question (*Armory* v *Delamirie* (1722) 1 Str 505), i.e. where the officer fails to produce the actual or a similar device and answer D is therefore incorrect.

Question 8

Answer **B** — It is not a dying declaration: the death is not the subject of the charge and the circumstances of the death were not the subject of the declaration and answer A is therefore incorrect. It is not part of the *res gestae*, in that the statement is not contemporaneous with the event, and it is not closely associated with an action or state of affairs and answer C is therefore incorrect. Lastly, it is not a statement made by the deceased as it is not a declaration against his own pecuniary interest or a statement made in the course of duty and answer D is therefore incorrect. The House of Lords has declined to extend the rule to declarations against penal interest (*Sussex Peerage Case* (1844) 11 Cl & F 85) stating that to do so would render an accused person liable to be tried on the strength of incriminating statements by a deceased accomplice.

Question 9

Answer **D** — There is a rule of law called presumption of regularity, which covers this point. This rule includes a presumption that mechanical and other instruments were in working order at the time of their use. For example, automatic traffic signals are presumed to be in proper working order unless the contrary is proved (*Tingle Jacobs & Co. v Kennedy* [1964] 1 WLR 638). This presumption assists the prosecution and answers A and C are therefore incorrect. As in all cases, the defence have to prove their point on the balance of probabilities only and answer B is therefore incorrect.

Question 10

Answer **C** — Where an accused faces more than one charge of a similar nature or where evidence of similar allegations is tendered in support of one charge, the evidence of one accuser may be admissible to support the evidence of another. The underlying principle is that the probative value (the usefulness of the evidence) of multiple accusations may depend in part on their similarity, but also on the unlikelihood that the same person would find himself or herself falsely accused on different occasions by different and independent individuals. There are cases in which evidence was admitted because features were identified which were so bizarre as to amount to striking similarity in the true sense. One of these cases is *Lanford v General Medical Council* [1990] 1 AC 13, which the outline of this question broadly follows. In that case the evidence of each patient was rightly admitted to corroborate the allegation of the other and therefore answers A and B are incorrect. Any comment made by the doctor would not normally be admissible, as it does not relate to the facts in issue, i.e. the assault and answer D is therefore incorrect.

Question 11

Answer **D** — Only treason, perjury and speeding require corroboration in law and answer A is therefore incorrect. A corroboration warning is no longer a requirement in cases of complaints of sexual offences, and answer B is therefore incorrect. It is a matter of discretion for the judge whether such a warning should be given and so answer C is therefore incorrect. In *R v Makanjuola* [1995] 1 WLR 1348, Lord Taylor LCJ gave guidelines in respect of the exercise of the discretion:

> It is a matter for the judge's discretion what, if any warning, he considers appropriate in respect of such a witness as indeed in respect of any other witness in whatever type of case. Whether he chooses to give a warning and in what terms will depend on the circumstances of the case, the issues raised and the content and quality of the witness's evidence. In some cases, it may be appropriate for the judge to warn the jury to exercise caution before acting upon the unsupported evidence of a witness. This will not be so simply because the witness is a complainant of a sexual offence nor will it necessarily be so because a witness is alleged to be an accomplice. There will need to be an evidential basis for suggesting that the evidence of the witness may be unreliable. An evidential basis does not include mere suggestion by cross-examining counsel.

Question 12

Answer **C** — This is a good example of what strikingly similar evidence is about. Clearly evidence given by the boys about incidents not subject to the charge is evidence of bad character and therefore not generally admissible. However, it would be allowed where its probative value in deciding if Phillips is guilty or not, outweighs the prejudicial effect the evidence would have on the defendant and answer A is therefore incorrect. The example used in the question is an illustration adopted by Lord Hailsham in *DPP v Boardman* [1975] AC 421 (at p. 454) of the man who commits repeated homosexual offences and whose victims all state that he was attired in 'the ceremonial head-dress of a Red Indian chief or other eccentric garb'. It should not be supposed that all similar fact evidence must reflect this degree of idiosyncracy. Everything depends on the unlikelihood of repetition being attributable to mere coincidence. It is not necessary that the previous behaviour was subject to a formal charge, even non-criminal behaviour can be given as 'similar fact' and answer B is therefore incorrect. As far as corroboration is concerned, the classic definition of corroboration is to be found in *R v Baskerville* [1916] 2 KB 658 (per Lord Reid):

> . . . evidence in corroboration must be independent testimony which affects the accused by connecting or tending to connect him

with the crime. In other words, it must be evidence which implicates him, that is, which confirms in some material particular not only the evidence that the crime has been committed, but also that the prisoner committed it.

The evidence of the boys is of similar fact, but would not extend to corroboration per this definition and answer D is therefore incorrect.

Question 13

Answer **B** — Evidence is likely to be admissible if it goes beyond mere evidence of a tendency to commit crime and has a crucial bearing upon the question whether the offence charged was committed by this particular defendant. In these cases the evidence of previous offences or actions of the accused *may be* admissible because they *connect* the defendant with the offence charged. The similarities between a series of occurrences will be used to justify an inference that the accused could not have acted innocently in respect of all of them, so that a defence which might have succeeded with regard to an isolated incident fails when other, similar incidents are brought into account. Answer A is therefore incorrect. Whereas evidence of the commission of homosexual acts is not necessarily prejudicial to an accused, the previous convictions would be on these facts. The question is broadly based on *R* v *Beggs* (1989) 90 Cr App R 430, where the evidence was not of convictions, but of the accused's homosexual tendencies. Clearly such convictions can be adduced prior to conviction and answer C is therefore incorrect. As far as losing the right not to have previous convictions introduced, this can only be done in limited circumstances. Those limited circumstances as outlined in s. 1(3)(ii) Criminal Evidence Act 1898 are:

. . . he has personally or by his advocate asked questions of the witnesses for the prosecution with a view to establish his own good character, or has given evidence of his good character, or the nature or conduct of the defence is such as to involve imputations on the character of the prosecutor or the witnesses for the prosecution or the deceased victim of the alleged crime.

This is not the case here and answer D is therefore incorrect.

Question 14

Answer **A** — Amongst the criteria for admitting a business document under s. 24 of the Criminal Justice Act 1988 are:

- that the information was received in the course of business;
- that the information contained in the document was supplied by a person (whether or not the maker of the statement) who had, or who may reasonably be supposed to have had, personal knowledge of the matters dealt with.

Both these points are contained in the question (note the maker of the document only has to have knowledge of the matters dealt with on the document, not whether the messages were true or not (*R v Rock* [1994] Crim LR 843, CA). Answer B is therefore incorrect. It is immaterial that the accused was not the maker of the document and answer D is therefore incorrect. Also, in relation to business documents, provided the criteria outlined above are fulfilled it is immaterial whether the witness is able to attend court or not — the document will be admitted and answer C is therefore incorrect.

Question 15

Answer **D** — In relation to non-expert evidence, the courts have allowed the following non-expert opinion evidence from a witness:

- identification of a person or object;
- the speed of a moving vehicle;
- evidence as to temperature or time;
- the value of an item (provided it does not require specialist knowledge to estimate the price).

One example of non-expert evidence that is likely to be given by police officers is provided by the case of *R v Davies* [1962] 1 WLR 1111: any competent witness may give evidence that in his or her opinion a person is drunk provided that he or she describes the facts on which his or her opinion is based. As can be seen this is not restricted just to police officers, but any competent witness. Statement 1 is incorrect and answers A and C are incorrect. Statement 2 is correct therefore answer B is incorrect.

Question 16

Answer **D** — Expert evidence will be appropriate in handwriting cases, and evidence of an expert witness may be admitted. It is for the judge to decide whether a witness is competent to give expert opinion and answer B is therefore incorrect. Section 81 of the Police and Criminal Evidence Act 1984 provides for regulations to be made requiring pre-trial disclosure. These rules, contained within Crown Court (Advance Notice of Expert Evidence) Rules 1987 (SI 1987 No. 716), require any party intending to produce expert evidence to furnish to the other parties in the proceedings a statement in writing of the expert finding. This allows the other parties to review the statement and, if necessary, call their own expert witness. (Note that this applies equally to the defence as it does to the prosecution and answer A is therefore incorrect.) A summary will not suffice and answer C is also therefore incorrect.

Question 17

Answer **C** — The courts may take what is known as 'judicial notice' of various matters that are so well known or clearly established that proof of them is not required. Judicial notice is another way of saying that a court accepts a fact or facts without formal proof.

Examples of this exception to the burden of proof include matters which are common knowledge, e.g. Acts of Parliament, and a celebrated example is the fact that a fortnight is too short a period for human gestation (*R v Luffe* (1807) 8 East 193). Consequently, answers A, B and D are incorrect.

Question 18

Answer **A** — Both statements are correct. The two examples are from the leading case on the use of the good character of an accused (*R v Vye* [1993] 1 WLR 471). In *Vye*, the Court of Appeal decided that where the defendant has not given evidence at trial but relies on admissible exculpatory (free from blame) statements made to the police, the judge should direct the jury to have regard to the defendant's good character when considering the credibility of those statements. Where an exculpatory statement was evidence in the case, the credibility of the defendant who had given that account was a matter of evidential significance requiring a direction to the jury. Note, however, that evidence of good character cannot by itself amount to a defence. As both examples are true, answers B, C and D are incorrect.

Question 19

Answer **D** — Evidence is likely to be admissible at court if it goes beyond mere evidence of a propensity to commit crime and has a crucial bearing upon the question whether the offence charged was committed by this particular defendant. In these cases the evidence of previous offences or actions of the accused *may be* admissible because they *connect* the defendant with the offence charged. If so, the evidence that he or she has a disposition to commit that kind of offence or act in a particular way is relevant because it makes it more likely that he or she committed the offence charged. Therefore the probative value of that evidence may outweigh any prejudicial effect it might have on the defendant's case. This is one of the basic principles relating to similar fact evidence. So evidence of non-criminal behaviour/bad character can be admitted and answers A and B are therefore incorrect. It is not circumstantial evidence as it is not evidence of relevant facts from which the facts in issue (the rape charged) may be presumed with more or less certainty and therefore answer C is incorrect. It is, however, 'similar fact' and is likely to be allowed. The facts of this case are similar to that of *R* v *Butler* (1986) 84 Cr App R 12 where such evidence was adduced.

Question 20

Answer **C** — Section 36 of the Criminal Justice and Public Order Act 1994 provides that inferences can be drawn from an accused's failure to give evidence or refusal to answer any question about any object, substance or mark which may be attributable to the accused in the commission of an offence. An inference may be drawn only where four conditions are satisfied:

- the accused has been arrested;
- a constable reasonably believes that the object, substance or mark (or the presence of the accused (s. 37)) may be attributable to the accused's participation in a crime (s. 36 (an offence 'specified by the constable') or s. 37 (the offence for which he or she was arrested));
- the constable informs the accused of his or her belief and requests an explanation;
- the constable tells the suspect (in ordinary language) the effect of a failure or refusal to comply with the request.

The interviewing officer is required to give the accused a 'special warning' for an inference to be drawn from a suspect's failure or refusal to answer a question about one of these matters or to answer it satisfactorily. However, as one of the four factors has not been met this becomes irrelevant and answer A is therefore incorrect. For similar reasons answer B is also incorrect. There does not have to be evidence linking the mark to the crime, simply that it may be attributable to the accused in the commission of an offence and answer D is therefore incorrect.

7 EXCLUSION OF ADMISSIBLE EVIDENCE

STUDY PREPARATION

There are few more frustrating experiences for police officers than having brought a person before the court and presented the evidence against them, only to have some of that evidence excluded.

This area of law has grown up partly through the common law decisions of the higher courts and partly through statute. And now there is the additional force of the Human Rights Act 1998 which has focused attention on the defendant's inalienable right to a fair trial and the attendant safeguards under Article 6.

Many of the occasions where admissible evidence is later excluded by the courts arise in suspect interviews or other occasions whereby the police officer(s) concerned say or do something that renders any response by the defendant unreliable or its introduction in evidence unfair. Therefore areas of confessions and oppression are key features in this chapter, as are the practical consequences of an exclusion ruling being made.

Question 1

DAILLY was interviewed by police officers in relation to a murder. During the interview, when asked if he had strangled the woman he nodded his head and said he was sorry. He did not, however, verbally state that he had committed the murder. The following day he took police to the scene of the murder and gave a running commentary on camera of what he had done, and demonstrated on a female officer how he had strangled the victim.

in relation to 'confession', which of the following statements is true?

[A] The reconstruction on camera would not be a 'confession' as it is not a PACE interview.

[B] The fact that he only nodded and said he was sorry is not enough to be a 'confession'.

[C] Both the actions in the interview and the reconstruction would be a 'confession'.

[D] A 'confession' could only have been made by a verbal admission that he had committed the murder.

Question 2

Confession evidence may be excluded on the grounds that it was obtained by oppression. In this context, which of the following statements is correct?

[A] A claim of oppression cannot be based on the nature of the person being interviewed, only on the actions of the interviewers.

[B] It will be for the prosecution to show, beyond reasonable doubt, that the evidence was not gained by oppression.

[C] A claim of oppression would apply where a suspect was inhumanely treated while being booked in at the custody unit, and later confessed on tape.

[D] Failing to comply with the PACE Codes of Practice during an interview will amount to oppression.

Question 3

Police officers are interviewing CAINE, who is a school teacher, in relation to an allegation of indecency with children. CAINE categorically denies committing the offences. One of the police officers says to him 'of course we will now have to visit the school, the head will have to know, how is that going to look for you?' Fearing that the police would do this CAINE confesses to the crime, which he did in fact actually commit.

If challenged at court, might the confession be deemed to have been gained by oppression and excluded under s. 76 of the Police and Criminal Evidence Act 1984?

[A] Yes, as there is a causal link between CAINE's decision to confess and the officer's comments.

[B] No, as the officers did not actually threaten CAINE with violence, nor treat him inhumanly or degradingly.

[C] No, as the officers are entitled to make such enquiries, and are simply informing CAINE of that fact.

[D] No, as the confession is true it will not be excluded, even it was held to have been gained by oppression.

Question 4

BLAKEMORE was arrested for murder. On being told that if he confessed he would be charged with manslaughter only, BLAKEMORE stated he had shot the victim in self-defence. BLAKEMORE then told the officers where to find the gun, which he had hidden in a hedge. The gun was found and at a second interview BLAKEMORE identified it as the one he had used, again because he believed he would be charged with manslaughter only. Ballistic evidence shows it was the weapon used. BLAKEMORE was charged with murder. At BLAKEMORE's trial the judge ruled that the confession obtained at the first interview would be excluded, as it was 'unreliable'.

In relation to evidence the police can now give, which of the following statements is true?

[A] The police can state that BLAKEMORE identified the gun, as this was during the second interview, which should be allowed.

[B] The police can state that they found a gun where BLAKEMORE told them to look, and that it was the gun used in the shooting.

[C] The police may not be able to make a connection between BLAKEMORE and the gun.

[D] The police will be able to state that BLAKEMORE said he had used the gun, as this was during the second interview, which should be allowed.

Question 5

TAYLOR is standing trial for an offence of burglary. During the burglary, where TAYLOR pretended to be a meter reader, witnesses noted that the offender spoke with a pronounced stammer, and used the term 'pal' significantly. Whilst being interviewed on tape by police officers, TAYLOR stammered and used the word 'pal' 25 times during a 20-minute interview. TAYLOR also confessed to the burglary. At the *voir dire* the judge excluded the confession when the defence submitted it had been obtained unfairly. The prosecution seek to have the evidence of the stammer, and the use of the term 'pal', admitted to show the connection between TAYLOR and the description obtained from witnesses.

Is it likely that this evidence will be allowed during the trial?

[A]   Yes, as it is evidence properly obtained and admissible for a specific purpose.
[B]   Yes, as it is similar fact evidence and admissible to connect TAYLOR to the crime charged.
[C]   No, if the confession is excluded then the entire interview will be excluded.
[D]   No, as it is not one of the 'facts in issue' it will not be admissible.

Question 6

Constable PRYCE is involved in an undercover operation relating to the supply of controlled drugs. The officer has been making test purchases from GLOVER; compiling evidence that GLOVER is a drug supplier. Intelligence has recently been obtained that GLOVER may also be involved in the supply of illegal firearms.

Which of the following is true in relation to the attempt to gain evidence of the supply of illegal firearms by GLOVER?

[A]   Constable PRYCE could encourage GLOVER to supply firearms the next time a drug purchase is made.
[B]   A covert human intelligence source (CHIS) could encourage GLOVER to supply firearms while making a drug purchase.
[C]   Any attempt to ask GLOVER to supply firearms may well be seen as entrapment and any evidence obtained would be excluded.
[D]   Any attempt to get GLOVER to supply firearms would not necessarily be entrapment, but safeguards would have to be observed.

ANSWERS

Question 1

Answer **C** — A confession is a positive action by and adverse to the person making it. The person must use words or some other method of communication (e.g. nodding his or her head to a question, or a video tape of the suspect taking police to a murder weapon) and answer D is therefore incorrect. Confessions do not include silence by a person. The confession does not have to be a pure statement of guilt and can include the answers to questions asked in interview which are *adverse to the defendant.* Also, a confession may be 'wholly or partly adverse' to the maker, with the result that a so-called 'mixed statement', which is part confession and part clemency, is a confession for the purposes of the Police and Criminal Evidence Act 1984 and answer B is therefore incorrect. In *Li Shu-Ling* v *The Queen* [1989] AC 270, the accused agreed to take part in a filmed re-enactment of the crime — the murder of a woman by strangulation. He gave a running commentary explaining his movements, which he demonstrated on a female police officer. It was held that the re-enactment was to be regarded as a confession and answer A is therefore incorrect.

Question 2

Answer **B** — A court can exclude a confession where it has been, or may have been, obtained by the oppression of the person making the confession. This means that there must be some link between the oppressive behaviour and the confession. So, for instance, if the confession was made *before* the oppressive behaviour, this would not justify exclusion and answer C is therefore incorrect. A failure to follow the PACE Codes of Practice is not of itself an automatic reason for excluding evidence. The courts have occasionally excluded evidence even where the relevant Code of Practice *had* been followed, i.e. it is possible that a court might conclude that the treatment had been 'oppressive' under all the circumstances even though the Codes of Practice had been followed. However, a breach has not (yet!) been held to be oppressive *per se* and therefore answer D is incorrect. The courts seem to take into account the nature of the person being interviewed. It was said in *R* v *Gowan* [1982] Crim LR 821, that hardened criminals must expect vigorous police interrogation and answer A is therefore incorrect. How a criminal is defined as 'hardened', and where the line between 'vigorous interrogation' and oppression lies, remains open to speculation.

Question 3

Answer **A** — It is a question of fact for the judge on each occasion whether a person's treatment was oppressive and whether there was any link between that person's treatment and his or her decision to make the confession. The legislation itself gives little guidance as to what will amount to oppression, but does help with regard to whether it is true or not. Section 76(2)(a) of the Police and Criminal Evidence Act 1984 states:

> the court shall not allow the confession to be given in evidence against him . . . (notwithstanding that it may be true).

Answer D is therefore incorrect.

For other assistance it is necessary to be guided by relevant case law. In R v Howden-Simpson [1991] Crim LR 49, the defendant was a choir master and the police had told him that if he did not make a statement they would have to interview all the members of the choir and this could disclose other offences on his part. This was held to be oppressive and the confession was excluded (answer C is therefore incorrect). Although inhuman or degrading treatment and the use or threat of violence (whether or not amounting to torture) will be oppression, lesser 'threats' will suffice and answer B is therefore incorrect.

Question 4

Answer **C** — This question shows what could happen where vital evidence is lost due to police impropriety (i.e. a clear inducement to confess), particularly where a false pretence has been used. The first interview was rightly excluded, and for the same reasons it is more than likely that the second interview would also be excluded. Answers A and D are therefore incorrect. In this case it will not be possible to show any connection between the suspect and the weapon and, unless there is some other evidence to link the weapon to the suspect, the case may fail. The reason is that it would not be possible to say that the police went to the location where the weapon was hidden without at least implying that the suspect had indicated that it was there when interviewed and answer B is therefore incorrect. All that can be said is that the weapon was found at the particular location, which could be accessible to any number of people, and that the scientific evidence shows it to be the murder weapon.

Question 5

Answer **A** — Dealing with answer D first, one of the 'facts in issue' in any case is that of identification. Clearly the peculiar voice patterns go towards proving the identification of the offender. They are a physical feature of the defendant and not affected by anything that may have been done or said which rendered the *content* of the interview inadmissible and as such would be allowed (answer D is therefore incorrect). Even where a confession on tape is excluded, it may still be admissible for other matters such as the fact that the accused speaks in a certain way or writes or expresses himself or herself in a particular fashion. In such a case it will only be that part of the confession which is necessary to prove the point that will be admissible and answer C is therefore incorrect. Similar fact evidence relates to evidence of previous convictions or actions which may suggest that the accused has committed the offence charged. This is not the case here and answer B is therefore incorrect.

Question 6

Answer **D** — In cases where officers are trying to obtain evidence of offences yet to be committed, the key question as to the admissibility of evidence is whether the actions of those involved in the 'trap' amount to those of an *agent provocateur*. This is likely where the undercover officer encourages or invites the accused to commit a crime they would not have otherwise committed and answer A is therefore incorrect. Prosecutions based on evidence obtained by entrapment conducted other than by police officers are also subject to the guidelines laid down in *R* v *Smurthwaite* [1994] 1 All ER 898. Section 78(1) of the Police and Criminal Evidence Act 1984 cannot be circumvented by the police using, as *agents provocateurs*, convert human intelligent sources who will not be called as witnesses and answer B is therefore incorrect. The Court of Appeal has made it clear, however, that evidence of undercover police officers, where it was alleged they had been acting as *agents provocateurs*, would not be excluded in circumstances where they had done no more than 'give the defendant an opportunity to break the law' of which the defendant had freely taken advantage (*Attorney-General's Reference (No. 3 of 2000)* [2001] EWCA 1214). So provided that the use of undercover agents is restricted and safeguards observed to prevent abuse, a person's right to a fair trial will not be infringed (*Teixeira de Castro* v *Portugal* (1998) 28 EHRR 101). The courts have accepted that undercover operations may be the only way in which some people are ever brought to trial (*R* v *Latif* [1996] 1 All ER 353), and evidence might not be excluded — answer C is therefore incorrect.

8   DISCLOSURE OF EVIDENCE

STUDY PREPARATION

Once again, this is an area that began life as a common law development through the courts, being later encapsulated in statute — the Criminal Procedure and Investigations Act 1996.

Although most of the specific responsibilities under the Act fall on the disclosure officer, the general duties of the disclosure system are important to all police officers and others involved in the gathering of evidence.

As well as understanding the main principles of the Criminal Procedure and Investigations Act — and the Code that accompanies it — you should also understand the practical aspects of disclosure schedules, defence statements and retention of materials.

QUESTIONS

Question 1

There is a statutory duty imposed by the Criminal Procedure and Investigations Act 1996 to disclose material to the defence. Upon which of the following is that duty imposed?

[A] The Crown Prosecution Service.
[B] A police disclosure officer.
[C] A police investigating officer.
[D] A police officer in charge of the case (OIC).

Question 2

The Criminal Procedure and Investigations Act 1996 defines what is termed 'a criminal investigation' in relation to recording and retaining material. At which point in the following examples would the officers involved be deemed to be involved in 'a criminal investigation'?

[A] Officers are planning surveillance on premises but no suspect has been identified.
[B] Officers are keeping premises under observation with a view to identifying a suspect.
[C] Officers are keeping premises under observation and are observing a particular suspect.
[D] Officers are observing a particular suspect with a view to trying to discover whether a crime has been committed.

Question 3

Police officers have been keeping observations on a petrol station suspecting that an armed robbery will take place. Part of this operation involves videotaping the petrol station and the area surrounding it, and keeping a surveillance log. While engaged on the petrol station observations, the officers witness KHAN commit a series of thefts from unattended motor vehicles. They make original notes in their pocket notebooks of what they saw KHAN do, and they check the videotape which does not show anything of the thefts from the vehicles.

In relation to the case against KHAN, what do the prosecution have to disclose in order to comply with the Criminal Procedure and Investigations Act 1996?

[A] Everything they have as they are engaged on a criminal investigation.
[B] Only the surveillance log, as the tape does not show the thefts.
[C] The videotape must be disclosed or the case could be halted.
[D] Only the officers' pocket notebooks, with the original notes need be disclosed.

Question 4

LEE has been charged with murder, and is awaiting committal to the Crown Court. In relation to the unused evidential material held by the prosecution, how much, if any, needs to be disclosed prior to committal to ensure LEE's right to a fair trial?

[A] All of the unused material must be disclosed, or the case may be halted as an abuse of process.
[B] Some of the material should be disclosed at an early stage (e.g. information to assist a bail application).
[C] None of the material, as the Criminal Procedure and Investigations Act 1996 requires disclosure after committal only.
[D] Most of the material should be disclosed, except that material which has been deemed to be 'sensitive'.

Question 5

There is a statutory duty on the defence to provide a defence statement to the court and the prosecutor in connection with an indictable offence. Within what time limit must the defence statement be provided?

[A] 14 days prior to the trial commencing.
[B] 14 days after the committal proceedings.
[C] 14 days after receiving primary disclosure.
[D] 14 days after receiving secondary disclosure.

Question 6

By virtue of s. 5 of the Criminal Procedure and Investigations Act 1996, when a case is committed to the Crown Court the accused must give a defence statement to the prosecutor.

What information should be contained in that statement?

[A] Only the defence case in general terms.
[B] The exact nature of the defence case.
[C] The defence case in general terms and areas where they take issue with the prosecution.
[D] The defence case in general terms and areas where they take issue with the prosecution, and why.

Question 7

DAWLISH is giving evidence at the Crown Court as a prosecution witness. During DAWLISH's evidence-in-chief she gives evidence which is materially inconsistent with the first statement she made earlier to the police. In her first statement to the police DAWLISH stated that she had seen the accused at the place where the crime was committed about three hours before the crime was committed. This statement was contained in the schedule of unused material, but was not disclosed by the prosecution as it did not undermine their case. It is on her second statement to the police, which was disclosed, that she is now giving evidence.

What should the prosecution now do in relation to the first statement?

[A] Nothing, as disclosure rules ceased to apply when the trial began.
[B] Nothing, as the statement only supports the prosecution case, it does not undermine it.
[C] The prosecution should ensure it is retained, in case of any future appeal.
[D] The prosecution should disclose it immediately so that the defence can use it in cross-examination to discredit the testimony of the witness.

Question 8

Which of the following statements is true in relation to a 'disclosure officer' and his or her role and functions under the Criminal Procedure and Investigations Act 1996?

[A] The role must be performed by a regular police officer.
[B] The role must be performed by a police officer, who can be a special constable.
[C] The role can be performed by a member of support staff.
[D] The Crown Prosecution Service can perform the role, where appropriate.

Question 9

During a police investigation into a street robbery, a key eyewitness provides a statement outlining in detail the description of the attacker. When the robber is eventually captured, he admits the offence on tape and there is ample supporting evidence to show he is guilty. The key eyewitness's description, however, is completely different from the actual appearance of the accused.

Which of the following is true in relation to whether this statement should be included on the schedule and disclosed?

[A] The prosecution should disclose it if the disclosure officer considers it undermines the prosecution case.

[B] The prosecution should disclose it only if the prosecutor considers it undermines the prosecution case.

[C] The prosecution should disclose it only if the prosecutor and the disclosure officer agree it undermines the prosecution case.

[D] The prosecution should disclose it even if no one involved in the process considers it undermines the prosecution case.

Question 10

Constable CARPENTER is engaged in enquiries into an allegation of assault against BRODERICK. Constable CARPENTER obtains a statement from a witness that indicates that BRODERICK was not the person responsible for the assault.

What action best outlines Constable CARPENTER's responsibility as an investigator in relation to this witness statement as required by the Codes of Practice under the Criminal Procedure and Investigations Act 1996? Constable CARPENTER should:

[A] Retain the statement and include it on the relevant sensitive material schedule.

[B] Retain the statement and disclose it herself as it undermines the prosecution case.

[C] Carry out further investigation to gather further evidence that would assist the defence.

[D] Inform the prosecutor and seek guidance as to the correct procedure to follow.

Question 11

Constable SONG received anonymous information that stolen vehicles were being hidden in a garage. She attended the area one evening with Detective Constable GRANT in an unmarked police vehicle, which they used to keep observation on the garage. They saw NEWMAN pull up in a Range Rover and they approached him to question him about the car. On seeing them, he sped off and was lost. NEWMAN was traced two days later and was arrested. This was witnessed by MARTIN. Constable SONG became the disclosure officer, and subsequently discovered that Detective Constable GRANT was under investigation by the complaints department for giving false evidence in court in a recent case.

In relation to material that needs to be disclosed to the defence, which of the following is correct?

[A] A statement would have to be obtained from MARTIN and disclosed to the defence.
[B] The investigation against Detective Constable GRANT may have to be disclosed, even though he has not been convicted.
[C] The details of the police vehicle used for the observation would not need to be disclosed.
[D] As the anonymous information is inadmissible as evidence, the fact of its existence does not need to be conveyed to the prosecutor.

Question 12

SAVILLE was sentenced at court to a term of imprisonment of 18 months. However, owing to the length of time he had spent on remand and other factors, he was released after five months from the date of his conviction.

In relation to the retention of material as outlined by Criminal Procedure and Investigations Act 1996, which of the following statements is true?

[A] The material no longer needs to be retained as SAVILLE has been released.
[B] The material will need to be retained for a further month.
[C] The material will need to be retained for a further 13 months.
[D] The material will need to be retained for a further 6 months.

ANSWERS

Question 1

Answer **A** — The duty imposed by the Criminal Procedure and Investigations Act 1996 falls upon the prosecutor. In cases involving the police, the prosecutor is the Crown Prosecution Service (CPS). Although this could not be achieved without the assistance of the police, the duty is upon the prosecutor and answers B, C and D are therefore incorrect. While the duty of disclosure is placed on the prosecutor, the police have a responsibility to assist in this process. The Home Secretary's Consultation Document recognised the critical role of the police in an effective and fair disclosure process:

> There will be a heavy reliance on the investigator (the police) to identify material which ought to be disclosed, given the material itself will not necessarily be scrutinised by the prosecutor. . . . The investigator will also need to assist the prosecutor by telling him what he thinks are the issues of the case: the system demands a significant degree of liaison between the prosecutor and the investigator as a case develops and the issues in the case change.

All three of the roles performed by police officers outlined in the question bear the responsibility of this role.

Question 2

Answer **A** — The Criminal Procedure and Investigations Act 1996 Code of Practice under Part II of the Act outlines the definitions. Code 2.1 defines criminal investigations as:

> . . . investigations which begin in the belief that a crime may be committed, for example when the police keep premises or individuals under observation for a period of time, with a view to the possible institution of criminal proceedings.

In these cases the investigation may well have started some time before the defendant became a suspect and answers C and D are therefore incorrect. In order to satisfy the disclosure requirements, police officers should consider recording and retaining material in the early stages of an investigation. This would be the earliest stage, even before an actual operation had begun and answer B is therefore incorrect.

Question 3

Answer **C** — Clearly the officers' eyewitness account of the thefts would have to be disclosed, but what of the details of the surveillance which in effect was not part of the case in question? There is case law in relation to this. The prosecution only have to disclose material relevant to the prosecution in question, for instance surveillance logs concerning another matter would not need to be disclosed (*R v Dennis*, 13 April 2000, unreported) and answers A and B are therefore incorrect. The videotape, however, is a different matter. In *DPP v Chipping*, 11 January 1999, unreported, the prosecution failed to disclose that there was a closed circuit television at the site where the offences were alleged to have taken place. The police officers viewed the tape but felt that it had no use and it was destroyed. The court held that this information should have been disclosed. The result of this failure to disclose the evidence led to the case being dismissed as an abuse of process — answer D is therefore incorrect.

Question 4

Answer **B** — There has always been an ethical dimension to the duty to disclose, and the decision in *R v DPP, ex parte Lee* [1999] 1 WLR 1950 is an indication that it survives the introduction of the Criminal Procedure and Investigations Act 1996. In *Lee*, the Divisional Court considered whether the prosecution had a duty to disclose unused material in indictable-only offences prior to committal. The statutory framework for disclosure set out in the 1996 Act is silent as to any such duty until after committal. But there may well be reasons why it would be helpful to the defence to know of unused material at an earlier stage. For example, the following circumstances were considered by the court:

- the previous convictions of the alleged victim when they might be expected to help the defence in a bail application;
- material to help an application to stay proceedings as an abuse of process;
- material to help the defendant's arguments at committal;
- material to help the defendant prepare for trial, e.g. eye witnesses whom the prosecution did not intend to use.

Kennedy LJ said that a responsible prosecutor might recognise that fairness required that some of this material might be disclosed. Therefore only some of the material should be disclosed and answers A, C and D are therefore incorrect.

Question 5

Answer **C** — By section 5 of the Criminal Procedure and Investigations Act 1996, once primary prosecution disclosure has taken place and the case is committed to the Crown Court, the accused must give a defence statement to the prosecutor. The defence statement must be served within 14 days of the prosecution's compliance with the duty of primary disclosure. The court, however, may grant an extension entirely at its discretion, and may order further extensions on the same basis. As the time limit is from primary disclosure only, no other time is applicable and answers A, B and D are therefore incorrect.

Question 6

Answer **D** — The defence statement should outline the defence case in general terms. In addition, those issues, relevant to the case, which the accused disputes with the prosecution must be set out with reasons. This requirement to give reasons is intended to stop the defence going on a 'fishing expedition' to speculatively look at material in order to find some kind of defence. Because the defence statement must outline more than just a case in general terms, answer A is incorrect. The defence statement need not go so far as to set out the exact nature of the defence case (e.g. its oral cross-examination) and answer B is therefore incorrect. Note that the defence must outline where they are in dispute with the prosecution *and* state the reasons why and answer C is therefore incorrect.

Question 7

Answer **D** — There is duty on the prosecution to continue to review the disclosure of prosecution material right up until the case is completed (acquittal, conviction or discontinuance of the case) and answer A is therefore incorrect. Material must be disclosed if the prosecutor forms the opinion that there is material which might undermine the prosecution case or might reasonably be expected to assist the accused's defence. Even if the information did not undermine the prosecution case, the material might have to be disclosed and answer B is therefore incorrect. It is worth asking a number of pertinent questions. Would the previous statement bring the witnesses' credibility into question? Would this then assist the accused's defence? If the answer to both these questions is 'yes', the prosecutor would have to do more than just retain the information: it would have to be disclosed immediately to allow the defence an opportunity to effectively cross-examine the witness and answer C is therefore incorrect.

Question 8

Answer **C** — The Code of Practice to the Criminal Procedure and Investigations Act 1996 identifies certain roles within the disclosure process:

- prosecutor;
- officer in charge of the case (OIC);
- disclosure officer;
- investigator;
- supervisor of OIC and disclosure officer.

In addition, it is the responsibility of the chief officer of police of each force to put arrangements in place to ensure that the identity of the OIC and disclosure officer is recorded for each criminal investigation. The duty of disclosure falls therefore on the police, not the CPS as 'prosecutor' and answer D is therefore incorrect. The disclosure officer creates the link between the investigation team and the prosecutor and is therefore very important to the disclosure process. For investigations carried out by the police, there is no restriction on who performs this role. It could a police officer or, equally, the role could be performed by unsworn support staff (Code, paras 2.1 and 3.3) and answers A and B are therefore incorrect.

Question 9

Answer **D** — Where disclosure is required, the first task is to create a schedule of all *non-sensitive material* which may be relevant to the investigation and, which has been retained by the police but which does not form part of the prosecution case. Once the schedules have been completed, the disclosure officer must decide what material, if any (whether listed on the schedules or not), might undermine the prosecution case. The disclosure officer must draw this information to the attention of the prosecutor and the reasons why he or she believes that the material undermines the prosecution case. In addition to the schedules and copies of material which undermine the prosecution case, the Codes of Practice to the 1996 Act require the disclosure officer to provide a copy of any material, whether or not he or she considers it to undermine the prosecution case. One example of this would be a record of the first description of a suspect given to the police by a potential witness, whether or not the description differs from that of the alleged offender. Irrespective of any person's opinion, this material would have to be disclosed and answers A, B and C are incorrect.

Question 10

Answer **C** — Paragraph 3.4 of the Codes of Practice to the Criminal Procedure and Investigations Act 1996, requires investigators to pursue all reasonable lines of inquiry, *whether these point towards or away from the suspect*. Although the officer must retain the statement, it would not fit the definition of sensitive material (i.e. material which the investigator believes it is not in the public interest to disclose). Thus sensitive material does not mean evidence which might harm the prosecution case and answer A is therefore incorrect. It is the prosecutors' job to disclose the statement, not the police officers' and answer B is therefore incorrect. Answer D is avoiding the clear responsibility outlined in the Codes of Practice and is therefore incorrect.

Question 11

Answer **B** — What is relevant to the offence, and needs to be disclosed, is a question of fact. In *DPP* v *Metten*, 22 January 1999, unreported, the court held that the actual arrest for an offence was not relevant to the case as it did not fall within the definition of an investigation in s. 2(1) of the Criminal Procedure and Investigations Act 1996 and answer A is therefore incorrect.

Material obtained during an investigation does not have to be admissible in court for it to undermine the prosecution case (*R* v *Preston* (1994) 98 Cr App R 405) and therefore the anonymous information should form part of the schedule sent to the prosecutor and answer D is incorrect. Where officers have used an unmarked police vehicle for observation, information relating to the surveillance and the colour, make and model of the vehicle should not be withheld (*R* v *Brown* (1987) 87 Cr App R 52) and answer C is therefore incorrect. Disclosure of previous convictions and other matters, which affect the credibility of the witness, might undermine the prosecution case. Some guidance is given by the case of *R* v *Guney* [1998] 2 Cr App R 242. In *Guney*, the court said that the defence are not entitled to be informed of every occasion when any officer has given evidence 'unsuccessfully' or whenever allegations are made against him or her. However, in this case the court felt that disclosure should have been made. It will therefore be a question of fact in each case and consultation with the Crown Prosecution Service is advisable if there is any doubt.

Question 12

Answer **B** — Paragraphs 5.6 to 5.10 of the Codes of Practice to the Criminal Procedure and Investigations Act 1996 set out the retention periods where a person has been convicted. All material which may be relevant must be retained at least until:

- the person is released from custody or discharged from hospital in cases where the court imposes a custodial sentence or hospital order;
- in all other cases, for six months from the date of conviction.

If the person is released from the custodial sentence or discharged from hospital earlier than six months from the date of conviction, the material must be retained for at least six months from the date of conviction. So, in the circumstances of the fact pattern, the material needs to be kept for a further month to comply with the Codes and answers A, C and D are incorrect.

9 CUSTODY OFFICERS' DUTIES

STUDY PREPARATION

The duties imposed by the Police and Criminal Evidence Act 1984 on custody officers are many and various and, once again, there is no substitute for knowing them in detail. This is a big area, both in terms of its volume and its importance. The need to have custody officers at certain police stations, along with the exceptional circumstances when they will not be needed are key areas; so too are the basic entitlements of anyone when arrested and brought to a police station.

You will need to know the occasions and grounds on which some of a suspect's entitlements can be delayed and, of course, you will have to know the highly examinable areas of clocks, relevant times and time limits. A complex fact pattern containing different times, days and locations can often induce panic! However, once you have got the formula for working out the relevant times clear in your mind, detention periods and reviews are very straightforward and questions on them should represent 'easy marks'.

Reviews both before and after charge should be known, as should the areas of searching prisoners, seizing property and the treatment of people in police detention.

QUESTIONS

Question 1

Who has the responsibility, under s. 35 of the Police and Criminal Evidence Act 1984, to ensure that sufficient designated police stations are available in an area to deal with prisoners?

[A] The Police Authority for the area.
[B] The Home Secretary.
[C] The Chief Officer of Police for the area.
[D] The Superintendent/Commander for the area.

Question 2

In relation to the requirement to provide custody officers at police stations, under s. 36 of the Police and Criminal Evidence Act 1984, which of the following statements is correct?

[A] At least one custody officer must be appointed for each designated station, and a custody officer must be available at all times in such a station.
[B] At least one custody officer must be appointed for each station, but a custody officer need not be available at all times in such a station.
[C] At least one custody officer may be appointed for each designated station, but a custody officer need not be available at all times in such a station.
[D] At least one custody officer must be appointed for each designated station, but a custody officer need not be available at all times in such a station.

Question 3

Constable BEER has arrested HICK for criminal damage at the enquiry office of a non-designated police station, where she works alone. Constable BEER intends dealing with HICK at her own station, as he is only likely to be in custody for an hour. Constable BEER has called for assistance from Constable FRY, who works in a neighbouring station.

Would it be appropriate for Constable BEER to act as custody officer for HICK in these circumstances?

[A] Yes, provided she informs an on-duty Inspector of her intention.
[B] No, she is the officer in the case and must await the arrival of Constable FRY, who should act as custody officer.
[C] Yes, provided she informs an Inspector at a designated station of her intention.
[D] No, HICK may not be dealt with at a non-designated station.

Question 4

In which of the following situations would a person *not* be in police detention for the purposes of s. 118(2) of the Police and Criminal Evidence Act 1984?

1. PARSONS has been removed to a police station for his own safety under s. 135 of the Mental Health Act 1983.
2. GREEN is being detained after being arrested under s. 41 of the Terrorism Act 2000.
3. VERON is being detained after being served with a notice of detention under the Immigration Act 1971.

[A] Situation 1 and 3 only.
[B] Situation 2 only.
[C] Situation 2 and 3 only.
[D] Situation 1 and 2 only.

Question 5

McDOUGAL was detained for robbery and on his arrival at the police station his girlfriend was informed of his arrest. McDOUGAL was wanted for another offence of robbery in another police area and the custody officer intended to transfer him there when the enquiries were complete in relation to the first offence.

What does PACE Code C, para. 3.7 say about McDOUGAL's entitlement to have someone informed of his detention, because of his transfer to another station?

[A] His girlfriend must be informed of his transfer before he is moved to another station.

[B] He will be entitled to have someone informed of his detention on arrival at the second station.

[C] His girlfriend must be informed of his transfer after he has been moved to another station.

[D] He has no further entitlement to have someone informed of his detention as his girlfriend has been informed.

Question 6

HALL has been arrested for theft of a radio from a motor vehicle. HALL was arrested near the vehicle and he was accompanied by another person, who escaped the police. On his arrival at the custody office, HALL asked the custody officer, Sergeant HOSKINS, if he could make a telephone call. The arresting officer asked for this right to be delayed, as he believed HALL may try to alert his accomplice of his arrest.

Who would be able to authorise a delay of HALL's right to a telephone call in these circumstances?

[A] An Inspector may authorise such a delay.

[B] Only a Superintendent may authorise such a delay.

[C] Nobody, HALL has not been arrested for a serious arrestable offence.

[D] The custody officer may authorise such a delay.

Question 7

In relation to the denial or delay of a person's rights, under PACE Code C, which of the following statements, if either, is/are correct?

1. The maximum delay of a person's right not to be held 'incommunicado' in a non-terrorist case is 48 hours.
2. A person may be denied the right to a visit while in custody; the denial may be authorised by a custody officer.

[A] Statement 1 only.
[B] Statement 2 only.
[C] Both statements.
[D] Neither statement.

Question 8

CONNOR has been arrested for armed robbery of a building society, where £50,000 was stolen. The officer in the case has proposed that CONNOR be denied his right to have someone informed of his arrest, as it may alert his accomplice, who has not yet been arrested. The duty Superintendent is engaged at a firearms incident, but she can be contacted by mobile phone.

Would it be lawful for the Superintendent to authorise a delay to CONNOR's rights over the telephone in these circumstances?

[A] Yes, but the decision must be recorded in writing within 24 hours.
[B] Yes, but the Superintendent must attend the custody office in person as soon as practicable to confirm the decision in writing.
[C] Yes, but the decision must be recorded in writing as soon as practicable.
[D] No, the authorisation must be made in person.

Question 9

MARTIN was arrested for the kidnap and murder of a young girl. On his way to the police station, MARTIN made an unsolicited comment to DC BROCK that he had kidnapped another girl that day and that she was being held at a friend's house. On arrival at the station, MARTIN asked for a solicitor. DC BROCK requested an interview to be authorised immediately, in order to discover the whereabouts of the child.

If DC BROCK's request were granted, what should the custody officer do if MARTIN's solicitor were to arrive during the interview?

[A]   The solicitor may be allowed access, unless this would cause a risk to the kidnapped girl.
[B]   The authorisation will mean that the solicitor will automatically be excluded from the interview.
[C]   The solicitor must be allowed access to MARTIN as soon as he or she arrives.
[D]   An interview may not be authorised without a solicitor being present in these circumstances.

Question 10

KING was arrested at 10.00 am in Reading for an offence of theft. KING arrived at the police station at 10.15 am, when it was discovered that she was wanted for an offence of theft in Bristol. KING was interviewed and charged with theft, and at 3.00 pm the same day, she was taken to Bristol, to be interviewed, arriving at the custody office at 4.30 pm.

What would KING's 'relevant time' be, in relation to her detention in Bristol?

[A]   10.00 am.
[B]   3.00 pm.
[C]   10.15 am.
[D]   4.30 pm.

Question 11

Section 37 of the Police and Criminal Evidence Act 1984 allows a custody officer to detain a person without charge in certain circumstances, if he or she determines there is insufficient evidence to charge.

What points should a custody officer consider when arriving at such a decision?

[A] Whether or not the arrest was lawful and whether there is a need to secure or preserve evidence.
[B] Whether there is a need to secure or preserve evidence or obtain evidence by questioning.
[C] Whether or not the arrest was lawful and whether there is a need to secure or preserve evidence or obtain evidence by questioning.
[D] Whether or not there is a need to secure and preserve evidence only.

Question 12

PACE Code C gives guidance as to what a custody officer must record on a custody record when detaining a person with or without charge.

What details should be recorded on the custody record in these circumstances?

[A] The grounds for detention in the person's presence, unless it is apparent that he or she would not understand what was being said.
[B] The grounds for detention in the person's presence, regardless of his or her condition.
[C] The grounds for the person's detention which can be recorded at any time.
[D] The grounds for detention in the person's presence if it is practicable to do so.

Question 13

WEST, HILL and SANTOS have been arrested for criminal damage to a shop window. A witness saw one person from the group throwing a stone through the window, but was not able to identify the exact person who caused the damage. WEST has been interviewed by PC KEANE and the officer has asked the custody officer for him to be detained until the other two suspects are interviewed.

Under what circumstances may the custody officer detain WEST further in these circumstances?

[A]   WEST may be detained if the custody officer has reasonable grounds to believe it is necessary to preserve evidence.
[B]   WEST should be released as there is insufficient evidence against him to secure a conviction.
[C]   WEST may be detained if the custody officer has reasonable cause to suspect it is necessary to preserve evidence.
[D]   WEST may be detained until the investigation is complete against all three defendants.

Question 14

DENT was arrested for an offence of theft and taken to a nearby police station, arriving there at 2.00 pm. DENT's detention was authorised by the custody officer at 2.15 pm, and he was interviewed about the offence shortly after. DENT was released on bail at 4.00 pm, for further enquiries. DENT arrived at the station a week later at 2.00 pm, and his detention was authorised by the custody officer at 2.15 pm.

What is the latest time that DENT's detention should be reviewed, on the day when he returned to the station to answer his bail?

[A]   6.00 pm.
[B]   6.30 pm.
[C]   6.15 pm.
[D]   8.15 pm.

Question 15

BOWYER has been arrested for a serious arrestable offence. At 10.00 pm, DC HASSAN approached the custody officer, stating that he was not in a position to charge BOWYER and that a vital witness had been identified who would not be available until 9.00 am the following day. DC HASSAN asked if a Superintendent could authorise BOWYER's continued detention beyond 24 hours in order to speak to the witness. BOWYER has been in custody for 14 hours.

Could a Superintendent authorise such a request at this stage of BOWYER's detention?

[A] Yes, but only after he has been in custody for 15 hours.
[B] No, not until he has been in custody for 24 hours.
[C] Yes, but only after an Inspector has conducted a second review.
[D] Yes, provided an Inspector has conducted at least one review.

Question 16

Under ss. 43 and 44 of the Police and Criminal Evidence Act 1984, where a person has been in custody for 36 hours without being charged, the police must apply to a magistrate to extend a person's detention beyond that time.

What is the maximum amount of detention time that can be authorised by magistrates beyond the original 36 hours, before a person must be charged or released (do *not* consider offences under the Terrorism Act 2000)?

[A] 3 days.
[B] 72 hours.
[C] 36 hours.
[D] 60 hours.

Question 17

BRIARS has been in custody for 26 hours, having been detained under the Terrorism Act 2000. A warrant of further detention has been applied for and granted by a magistrate and BRIARS has returned to the custody office.

At what intervals should BRIARS now be reviewed in relation to his detention, and who should conduct the reviews?

[A] There is no requirement to conduct further reviews.
[B] Reviews should be conducted at least every 12 hours by an Inspector.
[C] Reviews should be conducted at least every 9 hours by an Inspector.
[D] Reviews should be conducted at least every 12 hours by a Superintendent.

Question 18

Section 40A of the Police and Criminal Evidence Act 1984, offers guidelines for officers of the rank of Inspector, when conducting reviews of people being detained without charge.

What does s. 40A say about whether such reviews may be conducted over the telephone?

[A] They may be conducted over the telephone in any circumstances.
[B] They may be conducted over the telephone, provided it is not reasonably practicable for the review officer to be present.
[C] They may not be conducted over the telephone in any circumstances.
[D] They may be conducted over the telephone if there is no officer of the rank of Inspector in the station where the person is being detained.

Question 19

CURSON has been arrested for harassment of her former boyfriend. She has been interviewed and the officer in the case, Constable HUQ has asked the custody officer for her to be released on bail, to allow further statements to be taken, before a decision is made whether or not to charge her. Constable HUQ has expressed concern that CURSON may commit further offences against her ex-boyfriend, and has asked that conditions be attached to her bail to prevent her from doing so.

If bail were granted for further enquiries without charge, under what circumstances may the custody officer attach conditions as requested by Constable HUQ?

[A] That there was a genuine risk of CURSON re-offending.
[B] That CURSON may interfere with witnesses in the case.
[C] That CURSON may interfere with witnesses or the administration of justice.
[D] Bail conditions may not be imposed in these circumstances.

Question 20

JANSEN has been arrested and charged with an offence of robbery. The custody officer has denied JANSEN bail, and he is being kept in custody for the next available court.

In relation to JANSEN's continued detention, when should reviews be conducted and by whom?

[A] By an Inspector, at least every nine hours.
[B] By a custody officer, whenever there is a change of duties.
[C] By a custody officer, at least every nine hours.
[D] JANSEN's detention must be reviewed only once by a custody officer, following charge.

Question 21

LOCKE was arrested for affray and on his arrival at the custody suite he was violent towards the custody officer. LOCKE was taken to a cell because of his behaviour and, because he had not been searched, the custody officer ordered him to be searched in the cell. The arresting officer, who was female, was present in the cell when LOCKE was searched by the male custody staff.

Have the provisions of s. 54 of the Police and Criminal Evidence Act 1984 (searching of detained persons), been complied with in these circumstances?

[A] Yes, a female officer may search a male prisoner, provided it is not an intimate search.
[B] Yes, provided the female officer did not conduct the search.
[C] No, the female officer should not have been present at the search.
[D] Yes, a female officer may search a male prisoner, provided it is not a strip search.

Question 22

PACE Code C, Annex A, allows for a person in police detention to be 'strip searched' in certain circumstances.

Who may authorise such a search for a prisoner in custody?

[A] An Inspector only.
[B] A Superintendent only.
[C] An Inspector before charge, and a custody officer after charge.
[D] A custody officer.

Question 23

CRAWFORD was arrested and taken to the custody office of a designated police station. The arresting officer told the custody officer that CRAWFORD had a warning signal on PNC, that previously, while in custody, she had concealed razor blades in her mouth and had used them to cause injury to herself. The custody officer decided that CRAWFORD's mouth should be searched for objects which she may use to harm herself.

Which of the following is true in relation to the search?

[A] The custody officer can authorise this search at the custody office.
[B] Only a Superintendent can authorise this search at the custody office.
[C] Only an Inspector can authorise this search at the custody office.
[D] Only a Superintendent can authorise this search at medical premises.

Question 24

EVANS was arrested for deception and was accompanied at the time by her boyfriend BOLTON. When he was interviewed at the station, BOLTON admitted that EVANS was in possession of a stolen credit card, which she had concealed in her vagina. EVANS admitted possession of the credit card, but refused to submit to a search.

Could EVANS be subjected to an 'intimate search' in these circumstances?

[A] Yes, but this could not be done by force.
[B] Yes, she is in possession of stolen property.
[C] Yes, and this may be done, if necessary, by force.
[D] No, an intimate search may not be authorised in these circumstances.

Question 25

PACE Code C, para. 12.2. provides a requirement for a detained person to have a continuous eight hour 'rest period' while he or she io in dctcntion.

When considering the 24 hours of detention, at what time does the calculation for a 'rest period' commence?

[A]   24 hours from the time of arrival at the station.
[B]   24 hours from the time of the last interview.
[C]   24 hours from the time of arrest.
[D]   24 hours from the time the detention was first authorised.

Question 26

In relation to the treatment and welfare of a detained person, under PACE Code C, which of the following statements, if either, is/are correct?

1.   A detained person should be given at least one light meal and at least one main meal in any period of 24 hours.
2.   When handing over the custody of a detained person to another officer, the custody officer still maintains responsibility for ensuring the person is treated in accordance with the Codes of Practice.

[A]   Statement 1 only.
[B]   Statement 2 only.
[C]   Both statements.
[D]   Neither statement.

Question 27

The Criminal Justice and Court Services Act 2000 allows for drug testing of detained people and for samples to be taken to ascertain if a Class A drug is in their body.

How long can a custody officer detain a person, after charge, in order to obtain the sample?

[A] Up to four hours, from the time the person was charged with the offence.
[B] Up to six hours, from the time the person was charged with the offence.
[C] Up to six hours from the time the sample was requested.
[D] There is no limit.

Question 28

BRIAR, aged 21, was arrested for theft and taken to the custody office, where she asked for her father to be informed of her detention. When the custody officer spoke to BRIAR's father, he informed her that BRIAR was suffering from a mental disorder, which would make it difficult for her to understand questions being put to her about the offence. BRIAR's condition was not apparent to either the custody officer or the arresting officer.

In relation to BRIAR's detentiion, what action should the custody officer now take?

[A] The custody officer must contact an appropriate adult, based on the information received from BRIAR's father.
[B] The custody officer must contact a medical practitioner to seek advice on BRIAR's condition before she is interviewed.
[C] The custody officer may decide whether or not an appropriate adult should be called, based on her own observations.
[D] The custody officer must contact a medical practitioner or a social worker to seek advice on BRIAR's condition before she is interviewed.

ANSWERS

Question 1

Answer **C** — The responsibility to ensure that sufficient designated police stations are available in an area to deal with prisoners, under s. 35 of the Police and Criminal Evidence Act 1984, is given to the Chief Officer of Police for the area. Answers A, B and D are therefore incorrect.

Question 2

Answer D — Section 36 of the Police and Criminal Evidence Act 1984 requires that one or more custody officers *must* be appointed for each *designated* station. As answer C states that such persons *may* be appointed, it is incorrect. Custody officers must be appointed at *designated* stations and therefore answer B is incorrect. It was held in the case of *Vince* v *Chief Constable of Dorset* [1993] 1 WLR 415, that a custody officer need not be available at all times in a designated station and answer A is therefore incorrect.

Question 3

Answer **C** — Section 30 of the Police and Criminal Evidence Act 1984 states that an arrested person should be taken to a designated station as soon as practicable after arrest. However, an arrested person may be dealt with at a non-designated station, provided the person is not likely to be detained for longer than six hours. Answer D is therefore incorrect.

Where a person is taken to a non-designated station, s. 36(7) states that an officer of any rank not involved in the investigation should perform the role of custody officer. However, if no such person is at the station, the arresting officer (or any other officer involved in the investigation), may act as custody officer. Answer B is therefore incorrect.

Where a person is dealt with in a non-designated station in the circumstances described, an officer of at least the rank of Inspector at a *designated station* must be informed. Answer A is therefore incorrect.

Question 4

Answer **A** — A person who has been detained under s. 135 of the Mental Health Act 1983, having been removed there for his or her own safety, or a person detained after being served with a notice of detention under the Immigration Act 1971, *will not* be in police detention for the purposes of PACE Code C.

A person who is being detained after being arrested under s. 41 of the Terrorism Act 2000, *will* be in police detention; therefore, Green is the only person *in* police detention in these circumstances. Consequently, answers B, C and D are incorrect.

Note that even though the others will not be in police detention, Code C, para. 1.12 makes it clear that such people must not be given treatment of a lower standard than other detained persons.

Question 5

Answer **B** — A person in police detention is entitled to have one person informed of his or her whereabouts as soon as practicable (PACE Code C, para. 5.1).

Under Code C, para. 3.7, if a person transfers to another police station, the same right applies on his or her arrival at the second station. This means that a person may have another person (or the same person), informed of his or her detention at the second station. Answer D is therefore incorrect.

There is no specific requirement for the custody officer to re-contact the person who was originally informed of the detention, either before or after the prisoner has been moved. Answers A and C are therefore incorrect.

Question 6

Answer **A** — Detained people are entitled to speak to a person on the telephone for a reasonable time or send letters. The right can be denied or delayed when a person has been arrested for a serious arrestable offence *or* an arrestable offence. Answer C is incorrect for this reason.

PACE Code C, para. 5.6 states that an officer of the rank of *Inspector* or above may authorise the delay if he or she has reasonable grounds for believing, amongst other things, that by allowing the person to exercise his or her right, it will alert other people suspected of having committed such an offence but not yet arrested for it. A Superintendent may authorise the delay, as well as an Inspector and therefore answer B is incorrect. A custody officer may not authorise such a delay (unless of course the custody officer is an Inspector). Answer D is therefore incorrect.

Question 7

Answer **B** — Statement 1 is incorrect. The maximum delay of a person's right not to be held 'incommunicado', in a non-terrorist case, is *36* hours. In terrorist cases it is 48 hours.

Statement 2 is correct. A custody officer has the discretion to allow, or deny, visits to people in custody. The reasons for denying such visits are a possible hindrance to the investigation and a lack of 'manpower' to supervise the visit (PACE Code C, para. 5.4 and note 5B).

Consequently, answers A, C and D are incorrect.

Question 8

Answer **C** — First, the Superintendent must be satisfied that Connor is in custody for a serious arrestable offence (which is the case in the fact pattern). Also, the Superintendent must have reasonable grounds for believing that if Connor were to exercise his right to have someone informed of his arrest, it may alert other people suspected of the offence, but not yet arrested.

PACE Code C, Annex B states that the grounds for action under this Annex shall be recorded and the person informed of them as soon as practicable. The authorisation can initially be made orally either in person or by telephone, but must be recorded in writing as soon as practicable. Answer D is therefore incorrect.

The decision must be recorded in writing *as soon as practicable*; therefore, answer A is incorrect.

Code C does not actually state that the Superintendent must attend in person in order to record the information in writing and answer B is therefore incorrect. Presumably, this means that in the age of networked custody computers, a Superintendent may confirm in writing without actually attending the custody office where the prisoner is held.

Question 9

Answer **A** — A Superintendent must be satisfied that Martin is in custody for a serious arrestable offence (which is the case in the fact pattern). Also, the Superintendent must have reasonable grounds for believing that to delay an interview will involve an *immediate* risk of harm to people, (PACE Code C, para. 6.6(b)(i)). Again, given the circumstances in the question, this is a reasonable assumption and answer D is incorrect for this reason.

If an interview is authorised in these circumstances (sometimes this is called an 'urgent interview'), it does not mean that the solicitor will be automatically excluded on his or her arrival and answer B is therefore incorrect.

When an interview has been started without the solicitor being present, he or she must be allowed to be present when he or she arrives, *unless* para. 6.6(b)(i) applies (i.e. the delay will involve an immediate risk of harm to people). Answer C is incorrect because of this exception.

Question 10

Answer **D** — Under s. 41(2) of the Police and Criminal Evidence Act 1984, a person's 'relevant time' is calculated from the time they arrive at the police station or 24 hours after they were arrested, whichever is earlier. Since most detainees arrive at the station well within 24 hours, their relevant time is generally when they first arrive at the station.

There are several variations contained within s. 41 of the 1984 Act, and the circumstances covered in the question are to be found in s. 41(5). Section 41 states:

> (5) If—
> (a) a person is in police detention in a police area in England and Wales ('the first area'); and
> (b) his arrest for an offence is sought in some other police area in England and Wales ('the second area'); and
> (c) he is taken to the second area for the purposes of investigating that offence, without being questioned in the first area in order to obtain evidence in relation to it,
> the relevant time shall be—
> (i) the time 24 hours after he leaves the place where he is detained in the first area; *or*
> (ii) the time at which he arrives at the first police station to which he is taken in the second area,
> whichever is the earlier.

Note that under s. 41(5), the detainee has, in effect, two detention clocks running. It is important to note that the second clock will start earlier if the detained person is questioned about the offence under investigation in the other police area. However, the detained person in the fact pattern was *not* questioned about the offence in the first station, and she arrived at the second station *less than 24 hours* after her departure from the first station. Her relevant time is, therefore, her time of arrival at the second station (i.e. 4.30 pm). Answers A, B and C are therefore incorrect).

Question 11

Answer **B** — Section 37 of the Police and Criminal Evidence Act 1984 places a duty on a custody officer to determine whether a person should either be charged, released with or without bail, or detained if there are reasonable grounds to believe that it is necessary in order to secure and preserve evidence relating to the offence for which he or she is under arrest, *or* to obtain such evidence by questioning. Answer D is incorrect, as a custody officer may detain a person for either reason.

The Divisional Court held that there is no express or implied requirement imposing a duty on a custody officer to inquire into the legality of the arrest and that the custody officer is entitled to assume that the arrest was lawful (*DPP* v *L* [1999] Crim LR 752). Of course, in light of the Human Rights Act 1998, if a custody officer is aware that an arrest may be unlawful, he or she would have difficulty defending a decision to detain a person subsequently. Answers A and C are therefore incorrect.

Question 12

Answer **D** — Under PACE Code C, para. 3.17, a custody officer should record the grounds for detention in the person's presence if it is practicable to do so. Therefore, in cases such as when a person is drunk or violent, it may not be practicable to record the grounds in their presence. Answer B is therefore incorrect. This recording of the grounds must, by virtue of Code C, para. 3.4, be before that person is questioned about any offence, answer C is therefore incorrect.

Answer A is incorrect. If a person cannot understand what is being said, it may be 'impracticable' to record the grounds for detention in his or her presence; however, it is not written as such in the Codes of Practice.

Question 13

Answer **A** — If the custody officer has determined there is insufficient evidence to charge, the person must be released unless the custody officer has *reasonable grounds for believing* that the person's detention is necessary to preserve or to obtain evidence by questioning the person (s. 37 of the Police and Criminal Evidence Act 1984). Answer C is incorrect as 'reasonable grounds for believing' requires a greater amount of evidence than 'reasonable cause to suspect'.

Although the person may ultimately be detained until all the suspects are interviewed in these circumstances, each case must be considered on its own merit, against the above criteria. Answer D is therefore incorrect.

Where the suspicion rests with several suspects, it may be appropriate to hold all suspects until they are all interviewed before deciding whether there is sufficient evidence to warrant a charge against any or all of them. Answer B is therefore incorrect.

Question 14

Answer **B** — An officer of at least the rank of Inspector must review a person's detention *at least once in the first six hours* of his or her detention. The person's 'review clock' will be calculated from the time that the custody officer first authorised detention. Where a person is released on bail, the 'review clock' will stop until he or she returns to answer bail. It will re-commence when the custody officer authorises detention on the second occasion.

In relation to the scenario, Dent's detention was authorised at 2.15 pm, which means that the first review should be conducted within six hours from that time. The time of his arrival, 2.00 pm, is irrelevant in terms of the 'review clock' (although it is significant in relation to his relevant time and overall period of detention). Dent was released on bail at 4.00 pm, so that on his return, he has 1 hour and 45 minutes on his 'review clock'.

Dent returned to the station at 2.00 pm, but again this time is irrelevant in terms of reviews, as his time in custody resumed at 2.15 pm. His review is due in 4 hours and 15 minutes (subtracting the original 1 hour and 45 minutes from 6 hours), at 6.30 pm. Answers A, C and D are therefore incorrect.

Question 15

Answer **C** — An officer of at least the rank of Superintendent can authorise a person's continued detention, beyond 24 hours, up to a maximum of 36 hours. The period can be shorter, but if a shorter period is granted, this can be extended up to the 36 hour limit.

The Superintendent must be satisfied that there is not sufficient evidence to charge, *and* the investigation is being conducted diligently and expeditiously, *and* that the person's detention is necessary to secure and preserve evidence or obtain evidence by questioning (s. 42 of the Police and Criminal Evidence Act 1984).

The extension of a person's detention must be made *within 24 hours* of the relevant time and answer B is therefore incorrect. Also, the extension cannot be granted before *at least two reviews* have been carried out by the reviewing Inspector. Answer D is therefore incorrect.

Although reviews are normally carried out after six and nine hours, they can be conducted earlier. Section 42(4) is deliberately worded, so that the focus is not on the length of time a person has been in custody, but on how many reviews have been conducted. Answer A is therefore incorrect.

A Superintendent could authorise an extension in these circumstances, but would have to wait until a second review had been conducted.

Question 16

Answer **D** — A Superintendent may authorise a person's detention without charge to a maximum of 36 hours (s. 42 of the Police and Criminal Evidence Act 1984). Any further periods of detention must be authorised by a magistrate.

A magistrate may initially authorise detention for 36 hours (s. 43). However, this period may be extended by 24 hours upon further application (s. 44), which means that a magistrate may authorise a maximum detention period of 60 hours. A person may not be detained for longer than 96 hours in total without being charged or released. Answers A, B and C are therefore incorrect.

Question 17

Answer **A** — Where a person is in custody for an offence under the Terrorism Act 2000, the first review should be conducted as soon as reasonably practicable after his or her arrest and then at least every 12 hours; after 24 hours it must be conducted by an officer of the rank of Superintendent or above. Once a warrant of further detention has been obtained there is no requirement to conduct further reviews.

Answer D would be correct only if the person was in custody prior to going to court for the warrant of further detention hearing. Answer B would be incorrect in any circumstances; once a person has been in custody for longer than 24 hours, having been arrested under the 2000 Act, his or her detention must be reviewed by a Superintendent. Answer C is incorrect as reviews of people detained under the 2000 Act must be conducted every 12 hours, following the first review.

Question 18

Answer **B** — The Criminal Justice and Police Act 2001 inserted s.40A into the Police and Criminal Evidence Act 1984, which will allow an officer of at least the rank of Inspector to conduct a review of detention before charge over the telephone, but only on occasions where it is not reasonably practicable for a review officer to be present at the station where the person is being detained. Answer C is therefore incorrect.

It is not intended that such situations should become a regular part of the reviewing process, and should be used only in limited circumstances. Answer A is therefore incorrect.

There is no mention in the 1984 Act about Inspectors working in particular stations, indeed, many reviewing Inspectors cover several stations containing detainees. Answer D is therefore incorrect.

Question 19

Answer **D** — Where a person has been released on bail without being charged, the custody officer cannot impose bail conditions (s. 47(1A) of the Police and Criminal Evidence Act 1984). Answer D is the only possible correct answer; therefore answers A, B and C are incorrect.

Question 20

Answer **C** — Where bail has been refused, the decision must be reviewed at least every nine hours by the custody officer. In practice, many custody officers operate the practice of reviewing a person's detention when they begin their tour of duty. This has the effect (on most occasions), of ensuring that a person's detention is reviewed every eight hours. While this is good practice, the Police and Criminal Evidence Act 1984 states that this must be done every nine hours where a person has been charged. Answer B is therefore incorrect.

The reviewing officer when a person has been charged is the custody officer and therefore answer A is incorrect.

Answer D is incorrect for the above reasons.

Question 21

Answer **B** — Under s. 54(9) of the Police and Criminal Evidence Act, 1984 the constable carrying out a search must be of the same sex as the person searched. Section 54 does not prohibit a constable of the opposite sex from being present at a search, provided it is not a strip search or an intimate search. Answer C is therefore incorrect.

Because of the prohibition referred to above, under s. 54(9), a constable may *not* search a person of the opposite sex, whether during an ordinary search, a strip search or an intimate search. Answers A and D are therefore incorrect.

Question 22

Answer **D** — Code C, Annex A, para. 10, outlines the need for strip searches to be carried out. The Police and Criminal Evidence Act 1984, however, outlines who may authorise such a search. Although not specifically mentioning strip searches s. 54 of the 1984 Act clearly outlines that it is the custody officer who authorises the searching of persons in police detention. Section 54(7) outlines the only exception to this, that is, intimate searches. This is the case before or after charge. As the authority of either an Inspector or Superintendent is not required, answers A, B and C are therefore incorrect.

Question 23

Answer **A** — An intimate search may be authorised by a Superintendent, and consists of the physical examination of a person's bodily orifices *other than the mouth*. The physical examination of a person's mouth is *not* classed as an intimate search, and may be authorised by a custody officer for the same reasons as a strip search. Answers B and C are incorrect as the search in the fact pattern does not amount to an intimate search.

An *intimate search* may be conducted only by a medical practitioner (or registered nurse), at medical premises, where the purpose of the search is to discover a Class A drug. Other *intimate searches* may be conducted at the custody office by police officers (provided all the criteria are met). Answer D is therefore incorrect for this reason.

Question 24

Answer **D** — An intimate search may be authorised by a Superintendent, and consists of the physical examination of a person's bodily orifices other than the mouth. The search may *only* be authorised when the authorising officer has reasonable grounds for believing that the person has concealed an article which could be used to cause physical injury or concealed a Class A drug which he or she intended to supply to another or export.

Since the search may be authorised only for the above purposes, answers A, B and C are incorrect. Where an intimate search is authorised correctly, reasonable force may be used (s. 117 and Code C, para. 8.9 of the Police and Criminal Evidence Act 1984). However, in these circumstances, the use of force is not permitted.

Question 25

Answer **C** — PACE Code C, para. 12.2, provides that a detained person must have a continuous eight hour 'rest period' while he or she is in detention; this period should normally be at night. The period should be free from questioning, travel or any interruption by police officers in connection with the case. Under para. 12.2, the period of rest may not be interrupted or delayed, except at the request of the person, his or her appropriate adult or his or her legal representative, unless there are reasonable grounds for believing that it would:

> (i)   involve a risk of harm to persons or serious loss of, or damage to, property; or
> (ii)   delay unnecessarily the person's release from custody; or
> (iii)   otherwise prejudice the outcome of the investigation.

The period of 24 hours is calculated from the time *the person was arrested*, and not from the time of arrival at the police station or when detention was first authorised. Answers A and D are therefore incorrect.

Answer B is incorrect, as on occasion, a person may spend 24 hours in custody without being interviewed. Although this may be rare, logic would suggest that the person must be allowed to rest during that period!

Question 26

Answer **D** — Statement 1 is incorrect. At least two light meals and one main meal shall be offered in any period of 24 hours. Drinks should be provided at meal times and upon reasonable request between meal times (PACE Code C, para. 8.6). Meals should so far as practicable be offered at recognised meal times (Code C, note 8C).

Statement 2 is incorrect. When handing over the custody of a detained person to another police officer, the custody officer *ceases* to have responsibility for ensuring that the detained person is treated in accordance with the PACE Codes of Practice and the responsibility passes to the person to whom the detained person is handed (s. 39(2)). Consequently, answers A, B and C are incorrect.

Question 27

Answer **B** — The custody officer may also detain a person after charge if he or she has reasonable grounds for believing that the detention of the person is necessary to enable a sample to be taken from him or her under s. 63B of the Police and Criminal Evidence Act 1984. For the purpose of obtaining such a sample, the custody officer may not authorise a person to be kept in police detention for a period exceeding *six hours beginning when the detained person was charged with the offence*. The time of charge and the time at which the sample was given must be recorded in the custody record (PACE Code C, para. 17.9). In these circumstances, answers A, C and D are incorrect.

Question 28

Answer **A** — PACE Code C, para. 1.4 states categorically that if an officer has *any suspicion* or *is told in good faith* that a person of any age is suffering from a mental disorder, is mentally handicapped, or is mentally incapable of understanding the significance of questions put to him or her, that person *shall* be treated as a mentally handicapped person for the purpose of the Code. There is no room for interpretation, and the custody officer must contact an appropriate adult in these circumstances. Answer C is therefore incorrect.

Although a custody officer may contact a medical practitioner or a social worker for advice as to how to deal with a person suffering from a mental disorder, Code C, para. 1.4 makes it clear that the information given by Briar's father is sufficient to ensure that a person is treated as such in these circumstances. Answers B and D are therefore incorrect.

10 IDENTIFICATION

STUDY PREPARATION

The area of identification was regulated by the Police and Criminal
Evidence Act 1984 and principally Code D of the Codes of Practice.
This is the starting point. However, identification is a very fertile area
for defence lawyers and, not surprisingly, case law in this area has
extended or restricted the legislation — depending on your view point.
One thing is certain — the case law has complicated the subject for
those who are trying to study it.

The law regulating the various methods of identification (e.g. witness
testimony, ID parades, DNA samples and fingerprints) should be
known and you should be able to recognise the relevant circumstances and authorisation levels that must exist.

QUESTIONS

Question 1

Which of the following best fits the definition of a suspect being 'known' as defined in PACE Code D?

[A] There is ample information known to the police to justify the arrest of a person for suspected involvement in the offence.
[B] There is ample information known to the police to give reasonable grounds to arrest a person for suspected involvement in the offence.
[C] There is ample information known to the police to give reasonable suspicion to arrest a person for involvement in the offence.
[D] There is ample information known to the police to justify the arrest a person for actual involvement in the offence.

Question 2

Constable BRANNIGEN was off duty when she witnessed a robbery; she tried to tackle the robbers but was knocked unconscious. Constable BRANNIGEN regained consciousness six hours later, and two hours after this she was interviewed by Detectives. She gave a description of one of the suspects, but named the other as MACKONICY, a well-known local criminal.

Which of the following statements is true?

[A] Constable BRANNIGEN's description of the suspects is not 'a first description' as it was given several hours after the incident.
[B] Constable BRANNIGEN may be shown photographs to help identify both the suspects.
[C] Constable BRANNIGEN may *not* be shown photographs to help identify the suspects, as she is a police officer.
[D] Constable BRANNIGEN's description of the suspects would be 'a first description' even though it was given several hours after the incident.

Question 3

STEVENS was involved in a fight, and Constable WRIGHT tried to arrest him. STEVENS escaped and Constable WRIGHT circulated his description. Constable WRIGHT resumed driving the police van. A short time later Constable WRIGHT was called to transport a prisoner. The prisoner was placed in the van and Constable WRIGHT was asked to identify the suspect as STEVENS, who had escaped earlier. This was because the arresting officer recognised STEVENS from the description circulated by Constable WRIGHT. Constable WRIGHT identified STEVENS as the person who had escaped, a fact STEVENS strongly denied.

Is this identification of STEVENS procedurally correct?

[A] Yes, provided Constable WRIGHT recorded the first description he gave.
[B] Yes, as the confrontation was unavoidable.
[C] No, STEVENS should have been kept away from Constable WRIGHT and an identification parade arranged.
[D] No, as Constable WRIGHT should not have been asked if he recognised STEVENS.

Question 4

Police officers investigating a robbery have obtained some forensic evidence and some video evidence that implicates four people. The officers have also obtained witness statements that state that the witnesses may well be able to recognise the suspects. The officers are convinced that the evidence they have is unequivocal and a conviction is likely.

In relation to identification parades, which of the following statements is true?

[A] The officers should hold a parade *only* if the suspects dispute the identification during interview.
[B] The officers should arrange an identification parade as a matter of course, as they have witnesses.
[C] The officers need not hold an identification parade as there is other evidence implicating the suspects.
[D] The officers need not hold an identification parade as there is video evidence implicating the suspects.

Question 5

SADDIQUE has been arrested on suspicion of robbery, and there are eye-witnesses available. SADDIQUE denies involvement and disputes the identification. He demands an identification parade. The local area has a very low percentage Asian population and the identification officer states that he will not run an identification parade, as it is unlikely that sufficient volunteers will be found. SADDIQUE's solicitor offers to find volunteers to assist.

In relation to these circumstances which of the following is true?

[A] The identification officer can proceed to other methods as he feels there is little chance in obtaining sufficient volunteers.
[B] The solicitor's offer cannot be accepted, the courts have held that such agreement is outside PACE Code D.
[C] The identification officer must at least take reasonable steps to obtain sufficient volunteers.
[D] The identification officer can proceed to other methods as he has reasonable grounds to suspect that it will not be possible to obtain sufficient volunteers.

Question 6

STEWART has been accused of rape and disputes identification. The investigating officer considers that a video identification would, *in the circumstances*, be the most satisfactory course of action to take as both an identification parade and group identification are not practical. The identification officer *may* show a witness a video film of a suspect.

In conducting the video identification the identification officer should ensure that, in addition to the suspect, at least how many other people are on the film?

[A] 8 people.
[B] 10 people.
[C] 11 people.
[D] 12 people.

Question 7

NGHANI is suspected of an offence of rape, and all relevant identification methods have been impractical to arrange. The identification officer is now arranging a confrontation with four witnesses, including the victim. NGHANI, however, has refused to take part in such a confrontation.

Can the confrontation now be held?

[A] Yes, as confrontation does not require the suspect's consent and reasonable force can be used under s. 117 of the Police and Criminal Evidence Act 1984.

[B] Yes, as confrontation does not require the suspect's consent and reasonable force can be used under the common law.

[C] No, as confrontation *does* require the consent of the suspect.

[D] No, as force cannot be used in any identification process.

Question 8

An armed robbery had taken place at a post office by a suspect wearing a mask to hide his features. The suspect demanded money, and this was recorded on video, which had a voice track. The post office worker who received the verbal threat, thought he recognised the voice as belonging to ROBB, a well-known local person.

In relation to voice identification, which of the following is true?

[A] The witness can give identification evidence of the voice, based on what he heard at the time.

[B] Only an expert witness can give voice identification evidence, based on the voice recording on the video.

[C] The jury should be allowed to hear the recording and compare it to the suspect's voice in court.

[D] Voice identification is not part of PACE Code D and is therefore inadmissible.

Question 9

BALLINGER was arrested on suspicion of burglary, as fingerprint identification from the scene of the crime was available. BALLINGER initially denied the offence, and the taking of his fingerprints was authorised to prove or disprove his involvement in the offence and taken for that purpose. Following further comparison and further interviews BALLINGER admits the offence. BALLINGER has been charged and the officer in charge of the case wishes to take his fingerprints and photograph. BALLINGER refuses this request.

Which of the following statements is true?

[A]   As BALLINGER has been charged, his fingerprints can be taken without his consent.
[B]   As BALLINGER has been charged, his fingerprints can be taken only *with* his consent.
[C]   As BALLINGER has refused, a Superintendent's authority, in writing, is required.
[D]   As BALLINGER has refused, a Superintendent's authority, which can be oral or written, is required.

Question 10

DYSERT was charged with an assault and had her fingerprints taken. At court, she was found not guilty of the offence, and she has no previous convictions.

What should now happen to DYSERT's fingerprints held on file?

[A]   The fingerprints must be destroyed as soon as practicable.
[B]   The fingerprints must be destroyed upon application by DYSERT.
[C]   The fingerprints can be retained and may be used in future police investigations.
[D]   The fingerprints can be retained but may not be used for future evidential purposes.

Question 11

Expert evidence in relation to fingerprints is admissible from suitably qualified individuals. How much experience in the field must such an expert have?

[A] 3 years.
[B] 4 years.
[C] 5 years.
[D] 6 years.

Question 12

DOHENY is standing trial for rape, and DNA evidence will be an issue for the jury. In relation to DNA evidence against DOHENY, which of the following is true?

[A] The DNA evidence will be sufficient to prove DOHENY was the assailant.
[B] The DNA evidence must be supported by other direct evidence.
[C] The DNA evidence can be supported only by other identification evidence.
[D] The DNA evidence can be supported by mere circumstantial evidence.

Question 13

Section 62 of the Police and Criminal Evidence Act 1984 allows for the taking, from a suspect, of an intimate sample. From whom can such a sample be taken?

[A] Any suspect in police detention.
[B] Any suspect in police detention suspected of committing a serious arrestable offence.
[C] Any suspect in police detention who was arrested for a serious arrestable offence.
[D] Any suspect in police detention who has refused to supply such a sample.

Question 14

In relation to intimate samples, which of the following statements is true?

[A] A registered medical practitioner must take all intimate samples.
[B] A registered nurse may take an intimate sample.
[C] A sample of urine is not an intimate sample.
[D] An intimate sample can be taken in the presence of a person of the opposite sex.

Question 15

EARNSHAW was charged with an offence of theft and a non-intimate sample (mouth swab) was obtained on 21 March. EARNSHAW pleaded guilty and was convicted on 28 March. On 2 April, the laboratory informed the officer in the case that the sample obtained after charge was 'insufficient' for analysis.

In relation to obtaining another sample, which of the following is true?

[A] Another sample can be obtained only with the consent of EARNSHAW.
[B] Another sample can be required, but must be before 2 May.
[C] Another sample can be required, but must be before 28 April.
[D] Another sample can be required, but must be before 21 April.

ANSWERS

Question 1

Answer **A** — The rules for identification differ between cases where the suspect *is known* and those where suspect is *not known*. PACE Code D 2.12, note 2E defines the term 'known' as where 'there is sufficient information known to the police to justify the arrest of a particular person for suspected involvement in the offence'. As soon as the police have information that would give good reason to arrest a suspect, they become 'known'. This good reason does not have to extend as far as reasonable grounds (therefore answer B is incorrect) nor reasonable suspicion (therefore answer C is incorrect), and is there to provide protection for the suspect. As soon as there are grounds to justify arresting the suspect, he or she should be arrested and afforded the rights to formal identification processes. Code D also states that it involves a suspect's *suspected* involvement in the offence, not his or her actual involvement and answer D is therefore incorrect.

Question 2

Answer **D** — PACE Code D requires that a first description provided of a person suspected of a crime (regardless of the time it was given) must be recorded (para. 2.2). This was the first description as given by Constable Brannigen and should be recorded in accordance with Code D. How strong the evidence would be, given the circumstances of the officer's head injury, would be a matter for the court, but Code D must be complied with and answer A is therefore incorrect. As far as showing photographs is concerned, one of the suspects is 'known' and therefore showing the officer photographs to identify both would be a breach of the Codes and answer B is therefore incorrect. Showing photographs of the accomplice, who is merely described, may be appropriate if the suspect is 'not known'. Code D provides for witnesses (including police officers) to be shown photographs or be taken to a place where the suspect might be for the purpose of identification (paras 2.26 and 2.28) and answer C is therefore incorrect.

Question 3

Answer **C** — It is essential that once a person becomes a 'known suspect', he or she is afforded the rights and protection provided by PACE Code D. In this case the second officer stated he recognised Stevens from the description given by Constable Wright and by

Code D 2.12, note 2E, this makes the suspect 'known'. It is important that any witnesses, *including police officers*, who might be used at an identification parade, are kept apart from the suspect. As this was not the case, the Codes were breached and therefore answers A and B are incorrect. As *any* contact could jeopardise a conviction, it is imperative the witness officer should not see the suspect. This risk is not reduced simply by not asking the officer if he recognised the suspect and answer D is therefore incorrect. In *R v Lennon*, 28 June 1999, unreported, a suspect was arrested for public order offences after his description was circulated by the police officers that witnessed the offence. After the suspect was placed in a van, the officers accidentally went in the van and identified the suspect. The court held that the person was a 'known' suspect and the identification evidence should have been excluded.

Question 4

Answer **B** — The House of Lords in *R v Forbes* [2001] 2 WLR 1 held that if the police are in possession of sufficient evidence to justify the arrest of a suspect, and that suspect's identification depends on eye-witness identification evidence, even in part, then if the identification is disputed, PACE Code D requires that an identification procedure should be held with the suspect's consent, unless one of the exceptions applies. The House of Lords went on to say that this mandatory obligation to hold an identification procedure under Code D, para. 2.3 applies even if there has been a 'fully satisfactory' or 'actual and complete' or 'unequivocal' identification of the suspect and therefore answers C and D are incorrect.

Despite the wording of Code D, it has been held that a suspect's right to have an identification procedure is not confined to cases where a dispute over identity has already arisen; that right also applies where such a dispute might reasonably be anticipated (*R v Rutherford* (1993) 98 Cr App R 191). If, for example, the police have arrested a suspect on the basis of other evidence, and there are witnesses who indicate that they might be able to make an identification, an identification procedure (or group identification etc.) should be arranged. A positive identification would strengthen the case for the prosecution; moreover defendants should not be deprived of the opportunity to have witnesses to the crime declare that the offender seen by them is not on the parade. The position may be different if the witness has already stated that he or she would not be able to identify the offender (*R v Montgomery* [1996] Crim LR 507) and answer A is therefore incorrect.

Question 5

Answer **C** — If the police fail to hold a parade when the suspect requests one, this is clearly a decision they may have to justify at the trial. In *R* v *Gaynor* [1988] Crim LR 242, the trial judge took the view that the police could have made a greater effort to find volunteers of Gaynor's racial group than they did, and he excluded evidence from a group identification that had been held in lieu. Whilst *Gaynor* may have been a perfectly valid decision on its own facts, the Court of Appeal in *R* v *Jamel* [1993] Crim LR 52 appears to have taken a softer line, holding that the defence could not object to the holding of a group identification if the holding of a parade (made up with mixed-race volunteers) might, in the circumstances, have taken weeks to arrange; in other words, 'impracticable' may mean impracticable within a reasonable timescale.

All reasonable steps must be taken to investigate the possibility of one identification option before moving on to an alternative, and an offer from a suspect's solicitor to find volunteers to stand on a parade is such a 'reasonable' step (*R* v *Britton and Richards* [1989] Crim LR 144). So belief on the part of the identification officer, even on reasonable grounds, is unlikely to satisfy the court and answers A and D are therefore incorrect. Clearly a solicitor's offer of help can be taken and answer B is therefore incorrect. Note, however, it is important to follow the guidance in the PACE Codes regardless of what agreement is obtained from the suspect or his or her solicitor. In *R* v *Hutton* [1999] Crim LR 74, the court said it was a mistake, whether it arose out of a request made by the defence solicitor or not, to have all participants on the parade masked.

Question 6

Answer **A** — PACE Code D, para. 2.4 states:

> The identification officer may show a witness a video film of a suspect if the investigating officer considers, whether because of the refusal of the suspect to take part in an identification parade or group identification or other reasons, that this would in the circumstances be the most satisfactory course of action.

The film must include the suspect and at least eight other people who so far as possible resemble the suspect in age, height, general appearance and position in life (Code D, Annex A, para. 2). The answer is therefore 'eight' and answers B, C and D are incorrect.

Question 7

Answer **D** — If carried out, a confrontation must be in accordance with Annex D to PACE Code D. The procedure has the advantage of not requiring the suspect's consent or co-operation (Code D, para. 2.13) and answer C is therefore incorrect. Code D does not state whether physical force may be used to make a suspect take part in a confrontation, but in *R v Jones, The Times*, 21 April 1999, the Court of Appeal refused to sanction the use of any such force and answers A and B are therefore incorrect. There is, however, judicial mistrust of confrontation, which can most clearly be seen in *R v Joseph* [1994] Crim LR 48. In *Joseph*, the police had done their best to arrange for identification procedures, but without success due to the suspect's appearance. The prosecution sought to proceed on the basis of other evidence, but the suspect demanded a confrontation, where he was identified by two of the witnesses. The trial judge admitted that evidence, on the basis that the defence had asked for the confrontation. The Court of Appeal took the view that the evidence was still fragile and excluded it under s. 78 of the Police and Criminal Evidence Act 1984.

Question 8

Answer **A** — At trial, evidence may properly be admitted from people who claim to have recognised the defendant's voice (*R v Robb* (1991) 93 Cr App R 161 and answer D is therefore incorrect. Although expert evidence may be adduced, it is certainly not limited to experts and answer B is therefore incorrect. If there are taped recordings of the offender's voice, expert evidence may also be admissible on the question of whether this matches the voice of the defendant. The jury should be allowed to hear any such recordings for themselves, so that they may form their own judgement of the opinions expressed (*R v Bentum* (1989) 153 JP 538), but no court room comparison is allowed and answer C is therefore incorrect.

Question 9

Answer **B** — Naturally a person can consent to having his or her fingerprints taken at any time; the law deals with occasions where such consent is missing. Such cases are covered by s. 61 of the Police and Criminal Evidence Act 1984. Under s. 61(3), fingerprints of a person detained at a police station may be taken without that person's consent in the following two circumstances (s. 61(3)):

- where an officer of at least the rank of Superintendent authorises them to be taken; or

- where the person has been charged or reported for a recordable offence *and* the person's fingerprints have not already been taken in the course of the investigation of the offence by the police.

Under s. 61(4), a Superintendent may only give authority for fingerprints to be taken if he or she has reasonable grounds:

- for suspecting the person is involved in a criminal offence; and
- for believing that the person's fingerprints will tend to confirm or disprove his or her involvement.

Such authority is not suitable *after* charge and answers C and D are therefore incorrect. The Superintendent's authority may be given orally or in writing, but if given orally he or she shall confirm it in writing as soon as is practicable (s. 61(5)). Note that the power to take fingerprints after charge applies only where the fingerprints have not previously been taken and answer A is therefore incorrect.

Question 10

Answer **C** — Until recently, under s. 64 of the Police and Criminal Evidence Act 1984, if the person from whom fingerprints are taken is cleared of the original offence, the fingerprints must ordinarily be destroyed as soon as is practicable. The Criminal Justice and Police Act 2001 has removed the requirement to destroy fingerprints of those persons who are not convicted and custody officers should no longer inform detained persons of the right to destruction and answers A and B are therefore incorrect. The 2001 Act removes this obligation in relation to fingerprints where the person is cleared of the offence for which the fingerprints were taken or a decision is made not to prosecute. The obligation to destroy is replaced by a rule to the effect that any fingerprints or samples retained can be used only for the purposes related to the prevention and detection of crime, the investigation of any offence or the conduct of any prosecution. This means that if a fingerprint match is established at a subsequent crime scene between an individual who has previously been cleared of an offence, the police are able to use this information in the investigation of the crime and answer D is therefore incorrect.

Question 11

Answer **C** — Fingerprint evidence should be presented by a qualified expert, with at least five years' experience in the examination and comparison of such evidence. Answers A, B and D are therefore incorrect.

Question 12

Answer **D** — DNA extracted from blood or semen stains, or even from body hairs, etc., found at the scene of the crime or on the victim is compared with samples (typically derived from mouth swabs) taken from the suspect. The process has been refined in recent years, but is essentially similar to that described by Lord Taylor CJ in *R* v *Deen*, *The Times*, 10 January 1994. A positive match between the two profiles does not necessarily provide comparable proof of guilt and the courts have made it clear that DNA evidence alone will not be sufficient for a conviction; there needs to be other supporting evidence to link the suspect to the crime and answer A is therefore incorrect. This may be any supporting evidence linking the suspect to the area or circumstances of the crime or may come from questions put to the suspect during interview. It would include circumstantial evidence, i.e. being seen in the area. It need not be direct evidence gained by other identification procedures or otherwise, answers B and C are therefore incorrect. In *R* v *Lashley*, 25 February 2000, unreported, in addition to the DNA evidence, evidence that the suspect had connections in the area was enough for the jury to consider the likelihood that the defendant was the assailant.

Question 13

Answer **A** — Before an intimate sample can be taken from a person in police detention, the consent of an officer of the rank of Superintendent is necessary, *together with the consent of the person* (s. 62(1) of the Police and Criminal Evidence Act 1984). Without the consent of *both*, such a sample cannot be taken and answer D is therefore incorrect. The taking of an intimate sample does, however, apply to those in police detention, and it is not further defined, i.e. it does not have to relate to serious arrestable offences and answers B and C are therefore incorrect.

Question 14

Answer **D** — The taking of an intimate sample need not be done by a registered medical practitioner and answer A is therefore incorrect. As a sample of urine is an intimate sample, answer C is therefore also incorrect. A registered nurse has no authority to take an intimate sample (contrast this with the power to carry out an intimate search) and answer B is therefore incorrect. Only where clothing needs to be removed in circumstances likely to cause embarrassment, in order to obtain an intimate sample, do the provisions set out in PACE Code D, para. 5.12, need to be followed. One of the provisions is that 'no person of the opposite sex may be present (other than a medical practitioner or nurse)'.

Question 15

Answer **B** — By s. 63A of the Police and Criminal Evidence Act 1984 a constable may require a person to attend at a police station to have a non-intimate sample obtained:

- where a person has been charged with a recordable offence or informed that he or she will be reported, or
- where the person has been convicted of a recordable offence

and, in either case, the person has not had a sample taken in the course of the investigation into the offence, or he or she has had a sample taken but it proved either unsuitable for the same means of analysis or the sample was insufficient.

The requirement to attend a police station must be made:

- within one month of the date of charge or of conviction; *or*
- within one month of the appropriate officer being informed that the sample is not suitable or has proved insufficient for analysis.

As it is 'or', the requirement runs to the latest date in the fact pattern — 2 May — and answers C and D are therefore incorrect.

Answer A is incorrect because it is unnecessary to obtain the consent of a person convicted of an offence and a person can be arrested for failing to comply with the requirement.

11 INTERVIEWS

STUDY PREPARATION

Another area of direct practical relevance to all police officers is that of interviews of suspects. This area is heavily regulated by the Police and Criminal Evidence Act 1984 and the Codes of Practice.

Key aspects of this area are:

- cautioning
- interview procedure at police stations and elsewhere
- access to legal advisers
- interviews with vulnerable people, the use of interpreters and emergency interviews

QUESTIONS

Question 1

MILLER was under police surveillance suspected of being involved in unlawful drug supply. MILLER was observed meeting another male and a large packet was placed in the boot of MILLER's vehicle. MILLER then drove onto a motorway and was followed by the surveillance officers. While on the motorway, officers from the traffic department stopped MILLER for speeding. The traffic officers lawfully search the boot of MILLER's vehicle and find the package. One of the officer's said: 'What's in the package?'

Would the question asked by the officer be an interview as defined by Code C of the Police and Criminal Evidence Act 1984?

[A] Yes, as the question criminally implicated MILLER.
[B] Yes, as officers were investigating MILLER for an offence.
[C] No, as the officers did not suspect MILLER of an offence at this stage.
[D] No, but MILLER would have to be informed that he was not under arrest and free to leave.

Question 2

An unsolicited comment made by a suspect and recorded in a police officer's pocket notebook may be admissible in evidence against them provided the PACE Codes of Practice have been complied with. In relation to the admissibility of such an unsolicited comment, which of the following is true? The comment:

[A] Is only admissible if signed by the suspect at the time.
[B] Is inadmissible if the suspect refuses to sign the note.
[C] May be endorsed by the suspect two days later and still be admissible.
[D] Need only be signed by the suspect, not necessarily the maker to be admissible.

Question 3

Police officers have been called by the principal of a High School to interview a juvenile who has caused damage to school property. The principal did not witness the incident, but wishes the juvenile to be interviewed on the school premises as the youth is due to sit a GCSE in two hours. The parents of the juvenile have been contacted, but are unavailable for some time.

Can the principal be the 'appropriate adult'?

[A]   In these circumstances only the principal can be the appropriate adult.
[B]   The principal can be the appropriate adult as the parents are not readily available.
[C]   The principal can be the appropriate adult provided the parents agree.
[D]   The principal will not be able to be the appropriate adult in these circumstances.

Question 4

MILLIGAN has been arrested on suspicion of a burglary that occurred one month ago and is being transported in the back of a police vehicle. On the journey MILLIGAN calls out to a passer-by, 'tell Jonesy the coppers have got me'. The officers are aware that there is another suspect outstanding and ask MILLIGAN to explain who 'Jonesy' is and where he is. MILLIGAN tells them. The officers then ask MILLIGAN where the outstanding property is, and if 'Jonesy' is guilty of the burglary.

Is this 'interview with a person who is under arrest' lawful?

[A]   No, such an interview can only be conducted at a police station.
[B]   No, as they did not stop the interview after they identified the location of 'Jonesy'.
[C]   Yes, as it was to clarify a voluntary statement made by MILLIGAN.
[D]   Yes, as there was property still to be recovered, and to facilitate the arrest of 'Jonesy'.

Question 5

A suspect has been arrested for possession of controlled drugs, and police officers have taken him to his home address to carry out a search. During the search some cannabis is found along with items of drug paraphernalia. A large sum of money has also been found.

In relation to the questions the officers can ask of the suspect at the scene, which of the following is true?

[A] Questions can only be asked relating to ownership of the items found.
[B] No direct questions can be asked, but any comments made should be recorded contemporaneously.
[C] The suspect could be asked where the money had come from.
[D] The suspect could be asked the location of other premises where drugs could be found.

Question 6

SCHIFFO has been arrested on suspicion of kidnapping and the victim is still missing. On legal advice, SCHIFFO exercised his right to silence throughout the interview. There is sufficient other evidence available and SCHIFFO is charged. After caution he says 'try as hard as you like, you won't find her where I have hidden her'.

In relation to the options open to the investigating officer, which of the following is correct?

[A] No action can be taken as SCHIFFO has been charged with an offence and cannot be further interviewed.
[B] The officer can re-interview but must caution the suspect as in PACE Code C, para 16.5 caution (old caution).
[C] The officer can re-interview and there is no need to re-caution SCHIFFO but simply remind him that he is under caution.
[D] The officer can re-interview and must further caution SCHIFFO as in PACE Code C, para. 10.4 caution (usual caution).

Question 7

McGUIGAN has been arrested and is about to be interviewed on tape. The custody officer tells McGUIGAN that his nominated solicitor refuses to attend, and asks if he wishes to nominate another solicitor or the duty solicitor. However, McGUIGAN declines to ask for the duty solicitor or another solicitor.

In the circumstances outlined above can the taped interview proceed?

[A] Yes, provided an officer of the rank of Inspector or above has given agreement for the interview to proceed in these circumstances.
[B] Yes, provided an officer of the rank of Inspector has given agreement and the suspect agrees in writing.
[C] No, as McGUIGAN has not stated that he has changed his mind over legal advice the duty solicitor must be called.
[D] Not unless delay will involve an immediate risk of harm to people or serious loss of, or damage to, property.

Question 8

POPOV is a Ukrainian national who is in police custody, and is being interviewed in relation to the offence for which he is under arrest. POPOV has his solicitor with him, as well as an interpreter, and he is being interviewed by Constable BRYANT.

Which of the following is correct?

[A] The interviewing officer is responsible for ensuring that POPOV can understand and be understood.
[B] The solicitor is responsible for ensuring that POPOV can understand and be understood.
[C] The custody officer is responsible for ensuring that POPOV can understand and be understood.
[D] The interpreter is responsible for ensuring that POPOV can understand and be understood.

Question 9

Constable ADAMS is dealing with an offence of theft. The suspect's solicitor has asked for pre-interview disclosure. Constable ADAMS tells the solicitor that he will disclose absolutely nothing at all, not even the date of the offence. On legal advice, the suspect remains silent during the interview.

In relation to the suspect's silence, which of the following is correct?

[A] The silence is likely to attract adverse inferences at court as there is no obligation to disclose any evidence prior to interview to prevent a suspect from lying.
[B] The silence is not likely to attract adverse inferences at court as although there is no obligation to disclose, the solicitor must be in a position to advise her client.
[C] The silence is likely to attract adverse inferences at court provided the interview is conducted properly.
[D] The silence is not likely to attract adverse inferences at court as the police must disclose prima facie evidence prior to interview.

Question 10

Detective Sergeant LANTZOS is carrying out a tape-recorded interview with a suspect for murder, and it is now a recognised mealtime. The interview is almost complete, two hours after it started, and the suspect will be released on police bail at its conclusion.

In relation to the correct procedure, which of the following is true?

[A] The officer must terminate the interview to allow the suspect to eat.
[B] The officer must take a short break of 15 minutes to allow the suspect to get refreshments.
[C] The officer can carry on with the interview, recording the grounds for continuing the interview on the tape, and then release the prisoner.
[D] The officer can carry on with the interview, recording the grounds for continuing the interview on the custody record, and then release the prisoner.

Question 11

HOUSE is being interviewed by detectives in relation to an allegation of fraud. During the taped interview, HOUSE alleges that his rights under PACE Code C were breached and that he wishes to make a formal complaint.

Which of the following is correct?

[A] The tape should be stopped and an Inspector summoned to deal with the complaint.
[B] The custody officer is responsible for deciding whether the interview should continue or not in these circumstances.
[C] The interviewing officer should make a note in his or her pocket notebook, and later, on the custody record, of the complaint.
[D] The custody officer should be summoned immediately, and the tapes left running until he or she arrives.

Question 12

BATES is in custody for an offence. She requested legal advice and was allowed to consult on the telephone with the duty solicitor. Shortly afterwards another solicitor, FRIEND, summoned by BATES's father, attended at the police station.

In relation to FRIEND, which of the following is correct?

[A] FRIEND must be allowed private consultation with BATES.
[B] BATES does not need to be told about FRIEND as she has already received legal advice.
[C] BATES must be told FRIEND is present and should be allowed a consultation.
[D] BATES does not need to be told about FRIEND as she did not request advice from him.

Question 13

WALLACE, who is from Glasgow, has voluntarily attended a police station in London knowing he is wanted for questioning in Glasgow. When contacted, Strathclyde Police state that they cannot send an officer and request that officer of the Metropolitan Police interview him and establish an address to allow service of a citation (summons). Strathclyde Police provide details of the incident to their colleagues.

In these circumstances which of the following is true?

[A] The Metropolitan Police officers cannot interview as only officers in forces bordering Scotland may conduct such an interview.
[B] When the Metropolitan Police officers conduct the interview, a PACE caution should be used.
[C] Where a Scottish caution is given by a Metropolitan Police officer, that officer should ensure WALLACE understands it.
[D] As under Scottish law WALLACE is not entitled to legal representation, the interview can proceed without a solicitor, even if requested.

ANSWERS

Question 1

Answer **C** — 'Interview' is defined by PACE Code C, para. 11.1A, as:

An interview is the questioning of a person regarding his involvement or suspected involvement in a criminal offence or offences which . . . is required to be carried out under caution.

Do the traffic officers suspect Miller's involvement in an offence? Code C, consistently with the common law, specifies that questioning a person only to establish his or her identity or the ownership of a vehicle or to obtain information in accordance with any relevant statutory requirements (for example, under the Road Traffic Act 1988) does not constitute an interview; nor does questioning which is confined to the proper and effective conduct of a search (*R* v *Gilbert* (1977) 66 Cr App R 237) and answer B is therefore incorrect. The wording of the question asked is vital. In *R* v *Miller* [1998] Crim LR 209, the court held that asking a person the single question, 'Are these ecstasy tablets?' criminally implicated the person and therefore the conversation was an interview — answer A is therefore incorrect. In cases where the person is not under arrest, certain information must be given to him or her. This is covered by Code C, para. 10.2 which states:

Whenever a person who is not under arrest is initially cautioned or is reminded that he is under caution (see paragraph 10.5) he must at the same time be told that he is not under arrest and is not obliged to remain with the officer . . .

As this is *after* caution answer D is also incorrect.

Question 2

Answer **C** — There will be occasions where suspects make 'unsolicited comments' implicating them in an offence before they are suspected of any involvement and therefore before they are cautioned (or further cautioned if already suspected). Such statements are likely to be admissible provided the PACE Codes of Practice are complied with. To comply with PACE Code C, para. 11.13 the suspect must either 'be given the opportunity to read that record and to sign it as correct' or 'to indicate the respects in which he considers it inaccurate' and answer A is therefore incorrect. Any refusal to sign the notes shall be recorded by the maker, but provided the note has been shown, such refusal would not exclude the comment and answer B is therefore incorrect. Code C, para. 11.13 goes on to say 'any such record must be timed and signed by the maker' and answer D is therefore incorrect. If the endorsement cannot be achieved straight away, it is no defence for the prosecution to argue that it was not practicable. This is demonstrated by *Batley* v *DPP, The Times,* 5 March 1998, where it was held that as Code C did not require an *immediate* endorsement and no time factor was laid down, there was nothing to constrain the police from returning the next day to get their endorsement.

Question 3

Answer **D** — Interviews at educational establishments should only take place in exceptional circumstances and with the agreement of the principal or the principal's nominee (PACE Code C, para. 11.15). This is the mandatory practice, however it is not mandatory that the principal be the appropriate adult and therefore answer A is incorrect. If waiting for the parents (or other appropriate adult) to attend would cause unreasonable delay, the principal can be the appropriate adult, and this is not dependent on the parent's consent and therefore answer C is incorrect. The only exception to this is where the juvenile is suspected of an offence against his or her educational establishment, as the youth is in the question. In these circumstances the principal cannot be the appropriate adult and answer B is therefore incorrect (Code C, para. 11.15).

Question 4

Answer **B** — The general rules for the conduct of interviews are contained in PACE Code C, para. 11.A: the suspect under arrest should be interviewed only about an offence at a police station. However, there are exceptions to this rule based on the necessity for the interview and answer A is therefore incorrect. Code C, para. 11.1(b) covers one of those exceptions, i.e. where delay would be likely to 'lead to the alerting of other persons suspected of having committed an offence but not yet arrested for it'. However, interviewing in these circumstances should cease once the relevant risk has been averted or the necessary questions have been put (para. 11.1). Code C, para. 11.1(c) outlines that interviewing would be lawful if delay would 'hinder the recovery of property'. One month after the offence would be unlikely to hold credence with the court. This together with the fact that questions could not be asked regarding

'Jonesy's' guilt make answer D incorrect. Clarification over a voluntary statement relates to prisoners being transferred between forces, i.e. no questions may be put to the suspect about the offence while he or she is in transit between the forces except in order to clarify any voluntary statement made by him or her (Code C, para. 14.1) and answer C is therefore incorrect.

Question 5

Answer **C** — The courts have recognised that there may be times when a person who is under arrest will be asked questions other than when at the police station. One such example is where the arrested person is present while officers search his or her home address and answer B is therefore incorrect. In *R* v *Hanchard*, 6 December 1999, unreported, the questions which were admissible included whether cannabis at the address belonged to the suspect and where a large quantity of money had come from (answer A is therefore incorrect). Where questions go beyond that needed for the immediate investigation it would be a breach of the PACE Code of Practice, clearly asking for evidence of offences unconnected with the search would be such a breach and therefore answer D is incorrect.

Question 6

Answer **B** — Once a person has been charged with an offence generally he or she cannot be interviewed about that offence. However, the rule that questioning must cease after the charge has exceptions and answer A is therefore incorrect. One of these exceptions is that questions may not be put unless they are necessary for the purpose of preventing or minimising harm or loss to some other person or to the public. The suspect must first be cautioned before any such questions are put and therefore answer C is incorrect. This caution is the one outlined in Code C, para. 16.5, i.e. 'he shall be warned that he does not have to say anything but that anything he does say may be given in evidence'. This caution is what is known as the 'old style' caution and answer D is therefore incorrect. The reason for this is that no inferences can be drawn from a refusal to answer these questions.

Question 7

Answer **A** — If legal advice has been requested, a legal representative must be present at the interview unless PACE Code C, para. 6.6 applies. This paragraph gives direction where solicitors have been contacted, but declined to attend. In such circumstances, if the person has been advised of the Duty Solicitor Scheme but has declined to ask for the duty solicitor, or the duty solicitor is unavailable, the interview may be started without further delay provided that an officer of the rank of Inspector or above has given agreement for the interview to proceed in these circumstances whether taped or otherwise. The suspect does not have to agree to this situation and answer B is therefore incorrect. This authority to interview granted by the Inspector is separate from the authority to interview granted by a Superintendent. Code C, para. 6.6 also outlines that a Superintendent can authorise an interview without a solicitor if delay will involve an immediate risk of harm to people or serious loss of, or damage to property. However this does not need to apply in every case, and where, as outlined in the fact pattern, the suspect effectively changes his mind about representation the interview can go ahead, answer D is therefore incorrect. Although the suspect can change his or her mind about legal advice, even where this is not the case (as outlined above) the interview can proceed and answer C is therefore incorrect.

Question 8

Answer **A** — It is the interviewing officer who is responsible for ensuring that the detained person can understand and be understood (*R v West London Youth Court, ex parte J* [2000] 1 All ER 823), and only the interviewing officer. Answers B, C and D are therefore incorrect.

Question 9

Answer **B** — There is case law in this area, which gives some guidance. Although adverse inferences may be drawn where there has not been full disclosure, in *R v Argent* [1997] Crim LR 346 it was held that there must be some disclosure (it would be for the jury to decide whether the failure to answer questions was reasonable). This disclosure should be sufficient for proper legal advice (*R v Roble* [1997] Crim LR 449). In *R v Imran* [1997] Crim LR 754, the court held that it is totally wrong to submit that a defendant should be prevented from lying by being presented with the whole of the evidence against him or her prior to the interview and answer D is therefore incorrect. As to answer A, the failure of the police to disclose relevant information when asked to do so by the accused or his or her legal adviser must be a factor capable of affecting the aptness of drawing an inference. If little information is disclosed, it is likely to be particularly difficult to draw adverse inferences. Moreover the accused can be penalised only for his or her failure to mention 'a fact', so that his or her failure to put forward a theory or speculation is not relevant. If the prosecution fails to establish that the accused has failed to mention a fact rather than a theory, the jury should be directed to draw no inference (*R* v *B* *(MT)* [2000] Crim LR 181) and answer A is therefore incorrect. Answer C is also incorrect for this reason.

Question 10

Answer **C** — Exceptions exist to the rule that breaks from interviewing must be made. These breaks are to be made at recognised meal times (PACE Code C, para. 12.7). Short breaks for refreshment must also be provided at intervals of approximately two hours. However, subject to the interviewing officer's discretion, a break can be delayed if there are reasonable grounds for believing that it would:

- involve a risk of harm to people or serious loss of, or damage to, property;
- delay unnecessarily the person's release from custody; or
- otherwise prejudice the outcome of the investigation.

It is the officer's choice and a break does not have to be taken (answers A and B are therefore incorrect). Any decision to delay a break during an interview must be recorded, with grounds, in the interview record (either on the written record or on the tape) (Code C, para. 12.11) and answer D is therefore incorrect.

Question 11

Answer **D** — If the suspect makes a complaint regarding his or her treatment since arrest, the interviewing officer must inform the custody officer and follow PACE Code C, para. 12.8. Paragraph 12.8 states:

> If in the course of the interview a complaint is made by the person being questioned or on his behalf concerning the provisions of this code then the interviewing officer shall:
> (i)   record it in the interview record; and
> (ii) inform the custody officer, who is then responsible for dealing with it in accordance with section 9 of this code.

Note it is recorded on the interview record and answer C is therefore incorrect. Code C, para. 9.1 states that 'a report must be made as soon as practicable to an officer of the rank of Inspector or above who is not connected with the investigation'. However, it is not necessary to stop the tapes; indeed, the tape should be kept running in accordance with Code E, note 4H and answer A is therefore incorrect. Code E, note 4H also outlines that 'continuation or termination of the interview should be at the discretion of the interviewing officer' and not the custody officer and therefore answer B is incorrect.

Question 12

Answer **C** — If a solicitor arrives at the station to see a suspect, the suspect must be asked whether he or she would like to see the solicitor *regardless of what legal advice has already been received* and regardless of whether or not the advice was requested by the suspect, answers B and D are therefore incorrect (PACE Code C, para. 6.15). Note that it is the suspect's choice whether to speak to the solicitor, who has no automatic right of consultation even if summoned by a relative and answer A is therefore incorrect. However, where a solicitor does arrive at the police station to see a suspect, that suspect has to be told of the solicitor's presence and must be allowed to consult with the solicitor should he or she wish to do so.

Question 13

Answer **C** — English and Welsh officers interviewing suspects in England and Wales when they are aware that the interview is required for a prosecution in Scotland, should comply with the PACE Codes of Practice, save that a Scottish caution should be used and answer B is therefore incorrect (the use of the English/Welsh caution may render the interview inadmissible in Scotland). Note that this applies to all such officers, not just those on bordering forces and answer A is incorrect. As the PACE Codes of Practice have to be complied with, the suspect is entitled to legal advice even though under Scottish law the suspect is not entitled to legal representation and therefore answer D is incorrect. In all circumstances officers should ensure that suspects fully understand the significance of a caution, even if it is not one they are used to.